BEHIND BARBED WIRE

Behind Barbed Wire

GERMAN PRISONER OF WAR CAMPS IN MINNESOTA

Anita Buck

NORTH STAR PRESS OF ST. CLOUD, INC.

Library of Congress Cataloging-in-Publication Data

Buck, Anita
    Behind barbed wire : German prisoner of war camps in
Minnesota / Anita Buck.
      144 p. 23 cm.
      Includes index.
      ISBN 0-87839-113-4 (alk. paper)
      1. World War, 1939-1945—Prisoners and prisons,
American. 2. World War, 1939-1945—Concentration camps—
Minnesota. 3. Prisoners of war—Germany. 4. Prisoners of war
—United States. 5. Minnesota—History, Military. I. Title.
D805.U5B83   1998
940.54'7273'09776–dc21   98-19434
                                           CIP

Copyright © 1998 Anita Buck

Second printing March 2000

ISBN: 0-87839-113-4

Printed in the United States of America by Versa Press, Inc., East
Peoria, Illinois.

Published by: North Star Press of St. Cloud, Inc.
                     P.O. Box 451
                     St. Cloud, Minnesota 56302

*This book is dedicated to
our daughters,
Carol Buck and Kitty Beal,
their husbands,
Robert Cullen and Scott Beal,
and our granddaughter,
Erika Beal,
in the fervent hope that they
may someday know a world at peace.*

Acknowledgements

To all who have aided me in gathering material for this book, I offer my very sincere gratitude

Special thanks go to the following for their help: Darla Gebhardt of the Brown County (Minnesota) Historical Society; Howard Hong of Northfield, Minnesota; Jo Ann Johnson of the Itasca County (Minnesota) Historical Society; Arthur A. Madow (now deceased) and Lyle J. Schreiber of the Rice County (Minnesota) Historical Society; Iris Mathiowetz of Red Wing; Mark Piehl of the Clay County (Minnesota) Historical Society, the Winona County Historical Society; John Drenth of Hollandale and Jim Loverink of the Hollandale Historical Society; June Lehman of the Renville County Museum; the library and newspaper staff of the Minnesota Historical Society; my husband Gene who proofed the manuscript; and to others who furnished answers to my questions, and made photographs available.

To Rita B. Dwyer and Corinne A. Dwyer of North Star Press of St. Cloud, Inc., I owe a huge debt of gratitude for their continued support and professional assistance in publishing *Behind Barbed Wire*.

Contents

Introduction

SUMMER, 1951. CAMP ATTERBURY, INDIANA. The 28th "Keystone" Division of the Pennsylvania National Guard was in training, called up for service during the Korean conflict. As an employee of Army Special Services, I was director of the main service club on the post. Because weekends were the busiest time at the club, my free days came at mid-week, a time when few others were off duty.

One day, I took a solitary hike to a remote section of the military reservation. There I discovered a tombstone, almost obscured by a tangle of grass and weeds. I pulled the undergrowth away, and found four more grave markers.

The inscriptions, weathered and lichen-encrusted, were difficult to read. I traced the carving with my fingertips, and made a startling discovery. The stones carried German names, one preceeded by the rank of "*Oberleutnant.*" Another was inscribed "*Obergefreiter.*" German ranks. How had German soldiers come to be buried in the middle of the United States?

On my return to post headquarters, I made inquiry about the small cemetery. At first there were no answers. At length I was referred to a groundskeeper who had lived in the area for many years. From him I learned that Camp Atterbury had been the site of a prisoner of war (POW) camp during World War II. It was the location for POWs eligible for repatriation—the sick and the wounded; protected personnel such as doctors, dentists, sanitation personnel, chaplains, and workers of volunteer aid societies, in excess of those needed to minister to the needs in camps for German Prisoners of War.

I visited the cemetery several times more, wondering about the men buried there. In midsummer most of the men of the 28th Division were reassigned. My enlistment was up. I returned to my home in Minnesota. The knowledge of the German POWs cemetery was filed in a remote corner of my memory.

November 1994. Stillwater, Minnesota. The *St. Paul Pioneer Press* "Q & A" column carried the following question: "America had a German prison camp in New Ulm, Minnesota, during the second World War, and after the war many German prisoners decided to stay in New Ulm. They liked this country better. How did that go over in New Ulm? Were they settled in, and how were they accepted?"

The answer: "Actually, none of the prisoners stayed in New Ulm after the war, according to Darla Gebhard, research director for the Brown County Historical Society. About 150 German prisoners of war, almost all enlisted men, began arriving at the camp on the outskirts of New Ulm in June 1944. The camp was one of seven of its kind in Minnesota. The prisoners worked on farms, in a canning factory at Sleepy Eye, Minnesota, and elsewhere throughout the area. Gebhard says all of the men were repatriated to Germany after the war. However, she says one of the ex-prisoners later did return to this country and settled in Wisconsin."

The item caught my eye and quickly brought to mind the cemetery at Camp Atterbury. I never really knew anything about the POWs in this country. How many were interned in the United States? Where were they located? What kind of facilities did they have? How were they treated? What effect did the presence of enemies of the United States have on the citizens? Curiosity compelled me to research the prisoner of war camps, concentrating on those located in Minnesota. I searched newspapers, Provost Marshal General records, historical society reports and tapes, and conducted personal interviews.

BEHIND BARBED WIRE

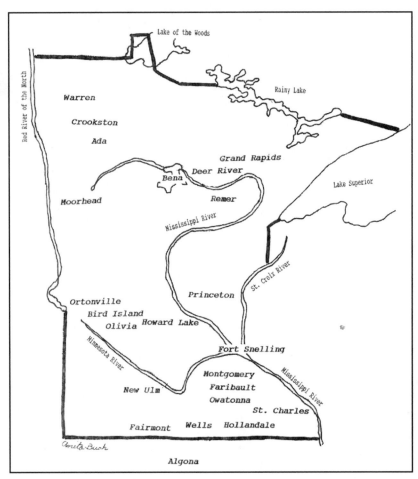

World War II German POW Camps in Minnesota

My purpose: to compile a record of prisoner of war camps in Minnesota. All the material is factual. Anecdotal material is reported as it was recorded by Army personnel, by reporters, and by people who were in contact with the POWs while they were in this country. I do not attempt to interpret history. I merely want to record it and preserve this facet of Minnesota history.

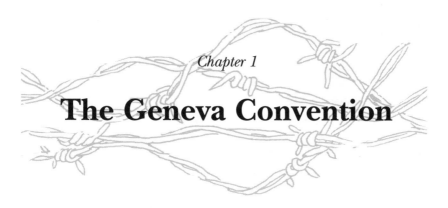

Chapter 1

The Geneva Convention

WORLD WAR II WAS TRULY A "WORLD" WAR, for it involved most of the nations on the globe. Battles took place on the continents of Asia, Africa, Europe, and in the South Pacific. Yet, except for an attempt by the Japanese to land on the Aleutian Islands off the coast of Alaska, the North American continent remained free from combat.

Still, the land areas of both Canada and the United States were involved in quite a different manner—the containment of prisoners of war (POWs).

On September 1, 1939, Nazi Germany invaded Poland and lit the match that exploded into a world conflagration. Without declaration of war, Adolph Hitler's airplanes began dropping bombs on thirty cities. On September 3, 1939, after years of unsuccessful attempts at appeasement, England declared war on Germany. That same Sunday afternoon, the last French ultimatum to the Germans expired, and the state of war automatically came into being. The United States made its formal declaration of war following the bombing of Pearl Harbor on December 7, 1941.

On the European continent, Axis soldiers captured by the Allies were shipped to England for imprisonment. Soon that small island was jammed with POWs. In August 1942, after much haggling, the United States agreed to accept 50,000 prisoners from Britain. The first of these arrived in this country in

November 1942. Camp McCoy, Wisconsin, which opened September 15, 1942, was one of the military sites selected for housing prisoners. By the spring of 1944, the United States was handling more German and Italian prisoners than there had been soldiers in America's pre-war army.

As the Allied nations were victorious in North Africa, Sicily, and Italy, shipments of POWs to the United States increased. Following the Normandy invasion in 1944, the numbers of prisoners escalated rapidly. In all, over 400,000 German prisoners of war were held in more than 500 prison camps in the United States. There were camps in every state in the union and in Alaska. These consisted of 155 base camps, which spawned numerous branch camps. One fifth of the base camps were located in the midwest.

Treatment of prisoners of war was governed by the articles of the Geneva Convention signed in 1929. The ninety-seven articles of that document spelled out the manner in which POW camps would be operated and how the inmates would be handled. Switzerland was designated to act as go-between for the United States and Germany to insure that the covenant of the Geneva Convention was followed.

The terms of the Geneva Convention dictated that prisoner-of-war camps had to be of the same standards as the base camps of the United States Army. The POW barracks at the camp in Flandreau State park on the Cottonwood River near New Ulm, Minnesota. A former CCC camp, the facility was typic l f other POW camps throughout the state. (Courtesy of the Brown County Historical Society, New Ulm, Minnesota)

To summarize the document, prisoner of war camps had to be of the same standards as the base camps of the United States Army. They could not be located within the 170-mile blackout area on either coast or near the Mexican or Canadian borders. They could not be located near munitions factories, shipyards, or vital industries.

Prisoners of war could be required to work for the benefit of their captors, but only physically fit POWs could be specifically requested to work. Officers were not required to work but could request employment if they wished. They still were to be paid, whether or not they worked. Non-commissioned officers could be used in supervisory positions only. Working hours for enlisted men could not be excessive. A reduction of earnings would be made for enlisted POWs not turning in a full day's work. A rest period of twenty-four consecutive hours per week, preferably on Sunday, was mandated. Prisoners could not be employed in any war-related work or in unhealthy, dangerous or degrading labor.

Food, medical care, clothing, exercise, and recreation had to be provided, with rations required to be equal in nutritional value to those served to the American troops. The diet for prisoners doing hard work was to consist of 3,400 calories per day. Moderate workers were to receive 3,000 calories, while non-working POWs were to be fed 2,500 calories.

W.D. Bell, senior field director for War Prisoners Aid in India, had traveled extensively in Europe and Asia monitoring camps maintained by both Allies and Axis nations. In a talk to the Kiwanis Club in Austin, Minnesota, on October 18, 1944, he emphasized that under the Geneva Convention there was a program of reciprocity between the warring countries. His work was to see that it continued. "When we provide Axis POWs in this country with equipment—sporting goods, instruments, craft materials, and so on—we are allowed to send a like amount of equipment to our own men held in enemy camps."

Civilian employees working in industries with prisoners of war were forbidden to communicate with them unless it was necessary for conducting business or unless given permission by the Commanding Officer of the prisoner of war camp. Unauthorized contact by civilians was considered an act of treason.

No physical punishment could be inflicted on a prisoner. If a man was not performing satisfactorily at a branch camp, he was returned to the base camp for punishment. Prisoners had to be protected from insult and public curiosity. Taking photographs of POWs was prohibited.

Publicity was to be used to inculcate in the public mind the proper understanding of prisoner of war activities and the role of civilians in their treatment.

Canteens were to be provided where prisoners could obtain personal items and snack foods, with purchases to be made with earnings from their employment.

Internees were allowed to elect a spokesman to act as liaison between the camp commander and the prisoners of war and to represent the POWs with the Swiss legation, International Red Cross, International YMCA, and other humanitarian organizations that oversaw their treatment. This provision was very important because German-speaking guards were a rarity, and few interpreters were available.

Prisoners of war processed in Europe were given superficial medical examinations and then assigned serial numbers. These were coded so the first component indicated the theater of war in which they were captured. A letter recorded the country in whose army the POWs served. The second component was the individual's number. The serial numbers were assigned consecutively.

The procedure was a little different for men who were processed in the United States. The first symbols gave the number of the Army Service Command, one through nine, into which the United States was divided. A "W" stood for War Department. A letter was included to indicate the country for which the captive had served. Serial numbers were very important because many prisoners had the same names. Many were misspelled or copied wrong.

Permanent record was made of personal and medical history, fingerprints, serial number, and place and circumstances of capture. Possessions were inventoried and returned to the POWs. Any money carried by a prisoner was kept by the United States government until the end of the war when it was returned. These records were forwarded to the International Red Cross and to Swiss authorities so the families of prisoners could be notified.

Prisoners of war were brought to the United States on ships returning from Europe and North Africa after delivering troops and materiel to the battlefronts. From North Africa collection areas, they traveled to reception centers at Casablanca, Morocco, and Oran, Algeria. Empty Liberty ships carried the POWs to the United States. The length of wait to be transported depended on the availability of shipping.

Once in this country, the POWs were put on trains and taken to various base camps around the country. En route many prisoners expected to see American cities bombed and in ruins. Contrary to propaganda they had been fed, they were amazed to see no sign of destruction from the war. They saw endless countryside, forests, flatlands, cities, villages, and cars everywhere. They were impressed by the beauty and the size of the country.

Each internee was issued blue work clothing with "PW" in white on the back of the shirt and coat. Each received a belt, two pairs of cotton trousers, two pair of wool trousers, gloves, wool coat, an overcoat, a pair of shoes, four pair of socks, four pair of drawers, four undershirts, a rain coat, and a wool shirt. German uniforms were to be worn in leisure hours.

When the prisoners first arrived in the United States, officers and enlisted men were kept at the same camps. Later they were segregated as it was discovered that trouble developed when the two were mixed. Even after the commissioned officers were removed from a camp and the enlisted men were asked to choose a leader as liaison between the prisoners and the Americans, the POWs always chose the highest ranking non-commissioned officer.

As noted earlier, contact with prisoners of war was restricted unless it was in the line of business or with special permission of the commanding officer of the camp. Dr. H.E. Schwermann of New Ulm, Minnesota, received permission to visit his brother Sergeant Willie Schwermann of the German Army, who was a POW at Hartford Camp near St. Joseph, Michigan. Willie told the doctor that he had received mail and packages regularly from his home. He said he got so much to eat in the POW camp that he had to go on a diet. The leader at Hartford was from Ulm, Germany, the city for which the American community was named.

At Camp Algona, Iowa, base camp for the Minnesota branches, copies of the Geneva Convention were mimeographed. Every American soldier and civilian serving at Algona and at all its branches received a copy. It was the intention that in dealing with prisoners of war, the provisions of the Geneva Convention would be followed to the letter.

Early in 1945, it became evident that American soldiers held captive in Germany were ill-treated, poorly clothed, and given little to eat. Public sentiment roiled against German POWs in the United States. A communique from Washington, D.C. on April 9 stated that the Army intended to stick to the provisions of the Geneva Convention in the handling of German POWs in spite of the reports. The War Department issued a statement saying, "The Geneva Convention established the basis for treatment of prisoners of war and has guided and will continue to guide the War Department with regard to its treatment of POWs."

That principle was followed until the last internee was returned to his homeland.

Chapter 2

Howard Hong,
YMCA Field Secretary

THE WORLD ALLIANCE OF YMCAs headquartered in Geneva, Switzerland, was qualified under the Geneva Convention of 1929 to promote educational and recreational facilities in prisoner of war camps. The YMCA had representatives in Europe, the Far East, Canada and the United States to mitigate the camp life of POWs. The work was carried on by mutual agreement among the United States, England, Germany, Korea, and Japan.

The United States was divided into four sectors—South, West, East, and the Midwest. The prisoners' aide for two-thirds of the Mississippi valley was Howard Hong. Born in Wolford, North Dakota in 1912, Hong received a B.A. from St. Olaf College, Northfield, Minnesota, in 1934. A conscientious objector to war, Hong

Howard Hong, May 24, 1995. Hong served as YMCA Prisoner's Aide during World War II. He assisted prisoners in redeeming their time with educational and cultural activities. His territory included Iowa, Missouri, Kansas, Nebraska, Wyoming, North Dakota, Wisconsin, and Minnesota. (Author's photo)

became an active pacifist in World War II. He worked for the World Alliance of YMCAs as field secretary for prisoners of war in Germany, Scandinavia, and the United States.

In America his territory ranged from Canada to Oklahoma, from Sheridan, Illinois, to the Rocky Mountains. This included Iowa, Missouri, Kansas, Nebraska, Wyoming, North Dakota, Wisconsin, and Minnesota. His work dealt not only with prisoners of war but also civilian prisoners, such as enemy nationals who as sailors or businessmen had been stranded in the United States. These were confined at Bismarck, North Dakota.

Hong's work differed from that of the Red Cross. In an interview in May 1995, Hong recalled the song of the 1940s—"Don't Fence Me In." He said that although prisoners were adequately fed, housed and clothed, they were still confined, which at best is a miserable way of life. In June 1944, Hong reported on his visit to the camp at Remer, Minnesota. "The men show contentment and resignation," he wrote. After the defeat of Germany, he noted "unusual defeatism by the leaders" at the Wells, Minnesota, camp. The YMCA provided books for all levels of reading. It had reading materials printed in German for POW use. The YMCA helped establish theaters, chapels, and athletics to occupy the internees during free time. It provided some materials and made others available for purchase. Arts and crafts equipment and materials, musical instruments, and sports gear were offered.

Said Hong, "The purpose of our work was to assist the prisoners in redeeming the time with educational and other cultural activities." In itself, a POW camp was a "center of impossibility," he said. The prisoners' aides helped to change that by making available something to facilitate a rewarding use of the prisoners' immense time. The presentation of a single guitar could result in a choir, for example, even an orchestra.

One of the programs sponsored by the YMCA was that of education. Among the POWs were many former teachers. Hong reported on July 24, 1944, that the camp at Cottonwood Park near New Ulm had teachers available for English, agriculture, history, and stenography. A medical officer had begun biology lectures. In January 1945, Hong observed that education at the

Fairmont branch camp was "meager but hopeful." There were classes in English, show card drawing, shorthand, and applied mathematics. A history class would begin when the text was received. The camp library had fifty books.

The captives were great scroungers. They made do with whatever they had. When they found wood they made furniture for day rooms. At one camp, Hong remembered, POWs used old tin drums to do metal work. At the Bena camp, he noted, the POW "expressed appreciation for work, beauty, healthfulness, and constructive activities." They had planted hundreds of trees, shrubs, flowers, and vegetable gardens in the camp.

In Nazi Germany, religion, to all intents, had been stamped out. In the POW camps, there seemed to be great interest in church services. Ministers and priests from community churches offered to conduct worship. Hong noted that at Faribault a Lutheran pastor preached every other Sunday, and a priest from Owatonna visited the camp fortnightly. Hong furnished an altar cloth and candles to be used on an altar made by the POWs.

The YMCA obtained various supplies, some of them out of the ordinary, for the camps. Once Hong sent in an order for materials to make wigs and beards. "Ridiculous," was the reply from the New York office supervisor. Hong explained that the wigs would be used for theatricals. Meanwhile, the making of the wigs would keep the men busy.

YMCA field secretary Hong made regular stops at all the camps, usually carrying books and musical instruments in his car for distribution. He visited the large base camp at Algona, Iowa, four or five times a year. He sent reports on his visits at branch camps to offices in New York, Geneva, and to the U.S. Army Provost Marshal. He made his own schedule of inspections. The needs of the branch camps became apparent during his visits; he did what was necessary as the conditions dictated. "It was a full time job," said Hong, "with plenty to do."

His first visit at the base camp at Algona was done shortly after the camp opened. At that time he left a violin, guitar, and books at the site. At Algona, Hong once was asked if he could arrange for a supply of concrete. He complied. With it the POWs built a huge, life-sized crèche complete with wise men and angel, sixty pieces in all. After the war, this was preserved by a group of residents of Algona. While not an artistic masterpiece, it still draws thousands of visitors every December. It is located in its own building at the county fairgrounds.

By October 1944, some 119 shipments of supplies had been received at Algona from the YMCA, the German Red Cross through the International Red Cross, from the Lutheran Committee for POWs, and the World Student organization.

As the prisoners earned money through their work in the canneries, agriculture, and lumber industries, they were able to buy various items—school books, musical instruments and music, study aids, sports equipment, and artistic supplies. Many of the POWs showed an interest in wood carving. On one of his trips, Hong found a sawmill near Fort Leonard Wood, Missouri, that made the butts for stocks of rifles. Some of the scrap were slabs of black walnut. Hong persuaded the mill operators to donate the material, then wrote out hundreds of address labels for each base camp and sent the wood to the POWs for their hobby.

Writing of his inspection at Montgomery branch camp on July 24, Hong noted that the town provided little in the line of recreation for the prisoners. They were able to swim in Lake Lexington, six miles away, when time and truck were available. The Lutheran minister lent twelve musical instruments to the camp. The POWs had improvised a horizontal bar and made lifting weights from cannery beet rollers. They fashioned a soccer ball from legging leather. On their own, the men had created jumping pits, a soccer field, and a fist ball court. They had procured tennis racquets and balls and were allowed to use a nearby playground. Hong left two fist balls, two soccer balls, a guitar, and two woodworking sets.

He wrote that although no classes were then being held at Montgomery, an English teacher awaited the arrival of the *Kleine Englische Sprachlehre* book with which he could conduct classes. Lutheran pastor the Reverend Beuhler and Catholic Father Skoblick held services in town for the internees.

The following month, Hong visited the facility at Moorhead. He reported that the men had made a fish pool—but had no books. He arranged to have a library shipped from Algona. He

German prisoners of war putting a roof on a barn on the Henry Peterson farm near Moorhead, Minnesota. (Courtesy of Henry Peterson Farm Papers, Northwest Minnesota Historical Center, Moorhead, Minnesota)

also managed to locate an electric washing machine for the POWs.

When Hong visited the camp at Howard Lake in August 1944, he learned that the prisoners had just been captured July 1 in Normandy. The men were so new to the Army and to captivity that they didn't know each other, so no programs had been planned at the branch. This group of POW was much older than those taken earlier, ranging from thirty to fifty years of age. They asked Hong to supply some YMCA books so they could begin classes in English, even though there was only one teacher among them. Hong noted that among the captives several men spoke Russian and Polish. During that visit, Hong left a guitar and a violin, four coping saws with two dozen blades, a volley ball, soccer ball, a pump, a wood carving set, a tool kit, and some games.

One of the activities arranged by the prisoners' aide was a sports festival scheduled for July and August 1944 at the Bena camp. The YMCA furnished medals, which had a space on the back where the winner's name could be engraved. Hong tried to get German Pentathalon medals for the event.

The YMCA sponsored a competition in painting and wood-working. Five branch camp prizes were offered with the best entries going to Algona for the final competition.

Sometimes when there were problems, Hong mediated between the prisoners and local people. Generally, though, civilians who came into contact with the POWs realized that the prisoners were people just as Americans were and treated the captives sympathetically.

Two complaints were registered at Owatonna during one of Hong's visits. The first was that the head man chose only the strongest POWs for work in the canning company in order to get a greater output. The weaker prisoners were not occupied as laborers, so earned nothing and only received their military pay.

The second problem had to do with a fire that occurred in January 1945. The three-storied nursery building in which the POWs were quartered burned down. The prisoners asked for compensation for their losses. Because they had no proof of what they had lost, the Swiss Legation was not able to support their demand for presentation to the American authorities.

Hong had few bad encounters in his work. He recalled just one incident when he thought his life was at stake. He arranged a visit in a branch camp in Wyoming. No guards were around when the German spokesman appeared with two other prisoners. The four went into a barracks to talk. Hong was sitting across from the three Germans. Suddenly they jumped up, lunging toward him. "For ten seconds, I thought I was a goner." Actually, the prisoners rescued him. A window that opened on hinges was fastened to the ceiling with a hook. The hook gave way, and the window was about to crash on his head. The trio of POWs caught it before it could hit Hong.

At various camps, the captives published German language newspapers for their own enjoyment.

Late in 1945, the United States State Department wanted someone from its staff to visit the camps. Hong was asked to show the representative around the branches. As, he kept to his regular schedule, the representative soon was tired of the rigorous pace Hong followed.

Lieutenant Colonel Arthur Lobdell, commander of the base camp at Algona, responsible for all of the branches, said that the war prisoners' aide program was the best thing that happened to the camps.

Summing up his service with the YMCA, Hong said, "The work had to be done here and in other countries. It was worth doing. So little was multiplied by the effect of the doing. One soccer ball, one book, and one guitar were passed around, and so affected many."

An incident that occurred after the war proved that the aide's work with the YMCA on behalf of the prisoners was remembered and appreciated. A friend of Howard Hong was traveling in Europe. At the Swiss border, he was stopped by a guard who was a former prisoner of war in the state.

"Are you from Minnesota?" asked the guard.

The answer was in the affirmative.

The guard asked, "Do you know Howard Hong?" He had happy memories of the effort put forth by the YMCA field secretary on behalf of the POWs.

After the war, Hong worked with displaced persons in Austria and Germany as well as with prisoners of war in the British zone. He continued in field positions until 1949. In 1972 Howard Hong was appointed director of the Kierkegaard Library at St. Olaf College in Northfield, Minnesota, where he taught philosophy beginning in 1938.

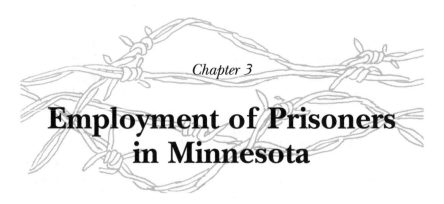

Chapter 3

Employment of Prisoners in Minnesota

SEVERE MANPOWER SHORTAGES OCCURRED in the United States during World War II because of the heavy transfers of men to the military. The War Manpower Commission (WMC), War Production Board (WPB), and War Food Administration (WFA) realized that with several hundred thousand prisoners of war in the country there was a plentiful source of labor. The three organizations initiated the prisoner employment program.

Farmers in Minnesota first felt the labor crunch in 1942. The WMC, WPB, and WFA realized that the logical area in which to place POW help was agriculture because it was not unionized. The captives would be in relative isolation in that type of work. Prisoners of war also could be used for contract labor in food processing and the logging of pulpwood and lumber products needed for the military, which was of the highest priority. The first prisoners were made available for contract labor in March 1943.

Housing for the POWs was a major concern. According to the Geneva Convention, prisoner camps had to be of the same standards as American Army camps. Earlier, in 1942, the Provost Marshal General submitted a plan outlining the use of abandoned Civilian Conservation Corps (CCC) camps, local fairgrounds, auditoriums, empty buildings, and tent cities as POW branch camps.

When a U.S. Army officer inspected the housing used for Mexican and Jamaican laborers at the Minnesota Canneries in southern Minnesota, he reported, "Due to sub-standard living conditions, we will not be a party to a violation of the Geneva Conference by placing the personnel in such quarters." Therefore, the plan suggested by the Provost Marshal General was put into effect.

Major W.L. Wolcutt, Omaha, chief of the POW branches of the Seventh Service Command, addressed a meeting of timber producers in Duluth early in November 1943. He told them of the availability of prisoners and explained that they were a last resort because of the scarcity of manpower. Wolcutt told the lumbermen that two side camps located at Olivia and Princeton the previous summer for farm crop harvests had worked out satisfactorily and encouraged the lumbermen to use POW labor.

Contracts were to be made between logging camp operators and the commanding officer of the prisoner of war camp. Railroad fare was to be paid by the contractor, and that sum would be deducted from the amount paid to the government for POW labor.

Applications for approximately 400 POWs were filed by producers in the Park Rapids-Cusson districts early in November.

As might be expected, there was resistance to employment of prisoners. Labor opposition halted plans to put POWs in larger southern Minnesota cities when wool, steel, and granite factories in Mankato sought prisoner labor. The same was true with the state hospital at Rochester.

Administrative problems, public animosity, and concentration of POWs in a few isolated camps hampered their use as workmen. Prisoners were to be used only where civilian labor was not available. Employers had to apply to the county agent or local WMC director to get certification of need. Employers had to provide adequate housing if no POW camp was available nearby. Employers were required to pay to the Army the prevailing wage rate in their area. The Army then paid the POWs a pre-set rate, generally eighty cents per day. The prisoner received chits worth ten cents, which he was able to spend at the camp canteen. The rest of the money was put into an escrow account to be paid to the POW when he returned to his own country.

POWs returning to camp after completing their work for the day. They were transported to and from the fields and factories by bus. Employers who applied for prisoner workders paid in advance for their labor and provided transportation. (Courtesy of the *Rochester Post Bulletin*)

Detailed contracts spelled out the work hours, pay scale, means of transportation, and provision for feeding the workers. Contractors had to adhere to the regulations reflected in the Geneva Convention of 1929. They had to avoid adverse publicity and provide orderly administration of the program.

A nine-member Farm Help Coordinating Committee was formed with Paul E. Miller, director of the University of Minnesota Agricultural Extension Services, as chairman.

The first application for farm help was submitted July 23, 1943. Odin J. Odegard, who had a 700-acre potato field near Princeton, Minnesota, asked for 100 POWs. The Army approved his request, and, as a result, Italians captured in Tunisia were sent from Camp Clark, Missouri. They arrived on September 5 and stayed until October 5. The POW worked at the Odegard warehouse and loaded trucks in the field. There was no opposition from residents of the area to the presence of the captives nor to the fact they were working for the firm. The prisoners performed satisfactorily to fill the need for laborers.

The situation was different in East Grand Forks. A plan to establish a POW camp there was abandoned because of a protest from the Grand Forks Trades and Labor Assembly. POW labor had been expected to be used in the True Foods Dehydrator plant. It was said that civilians would not work next to the men they bought war bonds to fight. Some area residents had had family members killed in the war and resented the presence of prisoners in their town. Major William Moiselle investigated the proposal. Although he found that construction workers were needed to build a warehouse, the request was denied because of civilian opposition.

The Timber Workers Union threatened strikes if POWs were used in logging. The CIO also objected. International Woodworkers of America Local 29, led by Ilmar Koivunen, provided opposition at Park Rapids. The prisoner plan there was foiled by threat of a strike.

Negotiations to establish a camp at Olivia for 100 captives to work at the Rogers Seed Company received community approval at a public hearing. Italian POWs arrived the first week of September and left October 14, 1943.

That year the use of prisoners of war for labor was mainly experimental. Then in fall 1943, production of pulpwood and paper was down. The shortage reached critical proportions because of the lack of manpower. It became obvious that the use of prisoner labor was an absolute necessity.

The first Minnesota contracts to employ POWs in logging were negotiated in November 1943, with timber operators at Osage, Laporte, Park Rapids, Morris, and Orr. Timber Workers Union Local 29 of the International Woodworkers of America in Duluth raised an outcry, and the plan was abandoned because of union opposition. Their objection: "It astounds us to think that men would be brought in who participated in taking American lives, to be housed in camps with electric lights, bathing facilities, clean sheets and bedding—conditions lumberjacks have been battling for seven years."

At length, contracts were signed with timber operators in Beltrami, Cass, and Itasca counties. POWs were housed in former CCC camps near Remer, Bena, and Deer River.

The first prisoners arrived in February and March 1944. Again Local 29 threatened to strike. The dispute was resolved in Washington, D.C., where officials determined that the labor shortage was genuine. Timber plants would have to shut down without the use of POW help. The War Department ordered that prisoners be put to work despite the objections of the union, and it was agreed that no POWs would be used in the unionized northeastern part of the state.

Some 100 German prisoners reached Duluth in February 1944, from Concordia, Kansas. They were transported to Remer and were housed in a former CCC camp. According to press and radio announcements, about 1,000 POW were expected to be at work in the woods in Northern Minnesota with headquarters in Bemidji, Duluth, and International Falls. A notice in the *Grand Rapids Herald-Review* on April 12 stated, "With a sense of relief, forestry officials learned that German POWs were to be used in aiding the effort to get a record cut from the Chippewa National Forest."

In January 1944, representatives of the Minnesota Canners Association met with the WMC officials and state extension services to discuss the use of POW in canneries. In March of that year, Army officers inspected possible housing facilities at Owatonna and Faribault. An advance unit of Germans arrived at Owatonna on March 23 to prepare the facility. Another branch camp opened at Moorhead in late May. The branch camps at Owatonna, Remer, Bena, and Deer River first were under the jurisdiction of Concordia, Kansas. In June 1944, they were transferred to the command of the new base camp at Algona, Iowa, which had opened in April.

An item in the *Mankato Free Press* May 27, 1944, stated, "While there are 100,000 prisoners of war in the United States, there is little prospect that any will be used in Blue Earth County. M.G. Knoff, Farm Labor Assistant for Blue Earth, says that imported labor will be Mexicans and Jamaicans."

"Seven prisoner of war camps in Minnesota, having 1,275 Germans, will supplement the state farm labor supply." This announcement was made early in June after Paul E. Miller, Minnesota Director for Agricultural Extension Service, and Dreng Bjornagaa, State War Manpower Commission, concluded arrangements with the United States Army and various employer groups. The POW were to be used on farms and in canneries.

Branch camps at Ortonville, New Ulm, Fairmont, Faribault, Montgomery, and St. Charles opened during June and July. Camps at Howard Lake, Bird Island, and Hollandale were activated in fall and were open only about two months. These prisoners were engaged in the canning industry. They were available to farmers only when their help was not needed in canneries. And farmers did indeed apply for prisoner workers. They paid in advance for their labor, provided transportation, and guaranteed a full day's work.

Rain in September delayed the potato and sugar beet harvest in the northwestern part of the state until the seasonal migrant workers—Mexicans and Jamaicans—had left. Growers obtained some 750 more German and Italian POWs. They were housed in Crookston, Ada, and Warren, Minnesota, and in Grafton and Grand Forks, North Dakota.

Employment of prisoners was of significant economic value even with the additional costs of providing adequate housing. Prisoners often were less efficient than regular labor. Even so, the Minnesota Canners Association said POWs were instrumental in harvesting and processing sixty-three percent of the 1944 corn and pea crop. The following year prisoners saved sixty-five percent of a record pea crop. In 1945 the Red River Valley faced an

Prisoners of war were instrumental in harvesting and processiong sixty-three percent of the 1944 corn and pea crop. POWs from the Whitewater camp near St. Charles, Minnesota, pitch pea vines into the chute of a viner. (Courtesy of the *Rochester Bulletin*)

emergency. Potato and sugar beets had to be harvested, but there were no workers. POW labor saved most of the potato crop, and thirty-four percent of the sugar beets.

Captive laborers were less effective in timber and pulpwood operations. Yet they cut thousands of cords of forest products.

In addition to logging, harvesting crops and working in canneries, captive workers also were employed in brick, tile and concrete factories, in poultry processing and in commercial ice and fish operations.

In all, some 1,275 German prisoners were allocated to Minnesota. Those billeted at Owatonna, Fairmont, and New Ulm stayed over the winter of 1944-1945. The rest returned to the base camp at Algona, Iowa, after completion of their contracts. They returned to Minnesota the following year to work in agriculture and lumbering.

By mid-April 1945, some POWs returned to the St. Charles and Faribault sites. A new branch camp was established at Wells in June. Other camps reopened in mid-summer to help harvest crops.

POWs worked in seven counties in 1944, in twenty-four counties in 1945. Most branch camps opened without protest from area residents, and residents accepted the presence of POWs. Many sympathized with their plight as victims of war. There were instances of POWs singing German lieder on their way to work, dropping propaganda leaflets, even painting swastikas on barns, which reminded people that the laborers were still enemy soldiers. Generally, though, residents adjusted to the presence of the POWs, and recognized the economic value of their labor.

Prisoners of war played a vital role in alleviating the labor shortages of the times because they kept the farms and industry running. By June 1945, their work had paid into the United States treasury some $22,000,000 in cash. The United States realized more than $102 million from POWs in the country, and over eighty million dollars was saved by the government through prisoner work. More than 140,000 Germans were engaged in agriculture, food processing, and the pulp lumber industry.

Said Paul E. Miller, head of the Farm Help Coordinating Committee, "Properly handled, the prisoners were a very important supply of labor."

Chapter 4

Princeton and the First Prisoners

MINNESOTA'S FIRST PRISONER OF WAR CAMP officially opened at Princeton on September, 1, 1943. The first contingent of POWs arrived there on Sunday, September 5, accompanied by forty United States Army military police. They were not Germans. These were 100 Italians captured in the Tunisian campaign. They had been off the battle fields just eight weeks.

O.J. Odegard of Princeton, owner of the Odegard Potato Farms, received a call Sunday morning announcing the arrival in the state of POWs from Camp Clark, Missouri. He motored to Elk River to meet commanding officer Capt. F.T. Mealey, then returned home to await the arrival of the captives in Princeton.

The POWs were brought to the village on a special train. From the depot, they were marched to trucks and taken to the Odegard farm ten miles northeast of the village. They exclaimed over the new sights and sang lustily as the trucks pulled away. Military Police followed in school buses.

According to the *Princeton Ledger* of Thursday, September 9, 1943, the Italians ranged in age from twenty to thirty-five. They were said to be "alert, clean-looking chaps in good spirits." Dressed in blue denim uniforms with "PW" on the back, the POWs carried rubber coats and hats. With them were two dogs brought along as mascots. The POWs were housed in an onion-drying shed recently constructed on the Odegard farm. Army

21

cots were provided, and a temporary kitchen was established. At roll call at least half of the POWs answered "Present" in English.

The citizenry was warned that POW rights were to be respected. They were cautioned that the Italians were not criminals; they were prisoners of war. A local priest, Father Adelbert Wagner arranged to hold early Sunday masses for the POWs.

On Monday morning, the captives went to work sprucing up the compound, cutting grass and setting up tents. The camp was surrounded by a fence with only the commanding officer, the guard on duty, and the medical officer allowed inside.

Food was brought daily from Fort Snelling. According to the *Ledger* the Italians were such good cooks that the MPs preferred to take their meals with the captives than at their own mess. The POWs received an extra camp quota of spaghetti.

Although the Geneva Convention specified that there should be no contact between prisoners and the public, that regulation was not strictly enforced at this, the first camp in Minnesota. Community leaders were allowed to tour the camp and were invited to stay for dinner. The *Ledger* reporter who accompanied the tour said they were treated to hamburgers, "the best this reporter has ever eaten."

Captain Mealey remained as commanding officer, with Lieutenent Glen H. Dietrich next in command. For the first few days, Captain J.V. Pischieri was the medical officer. After that, Odegard had to get medical help from Milaca or Princeton. Civilian doctor W.R. Blomberg made daily calls at the Odegard farm.

On September 23, one of the prisoners was injured. A truck going from the field to the camp ran off the road into a ditch. The POW suffered a fractured vertebra and was taken to Fort Snelling for treatment. Another was injured in a soccer game a few days later. Bones in his left leg were fractured, so he, too, was taken to Fort Snelling. These two were replaced by prisoners from Camp Clark, Missouri.

On November 4, the *Princeton Ledger* reported that O.J. Odegard and J.W. Thompson gave a dinner at the Princeton National Guard Armory on Friday for the POWs before they left the community. The Italian cook, whom Odegard called

"Charlie," presented Odegard with a large cake. It was decorated with an "OK," the nickname given to Odegard by the POWs.

On Saturday, their work in the potato field finished for the season, the Italian prisoners left Princeton to return to Camp Clark.

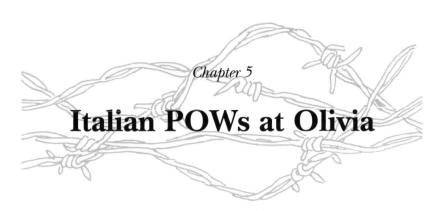

Chapter 5

Italian POWs at Olivia

IN 1943, ROGERS BROTHERS SEED COMPANY of Olivia, Minnesota, a producer of hybrid sweet corn seed, made application to the War Department for 100 POWs to relieve their labor shortage. The prisoners would be employed in harvesting and processing seed corn. Application was made first with County Agent Fred Giesler. The papers then were sent to the State Extension Service and from there to the War Department. Captain Charles M. Lee of Camp Clark near Nevada, Missouri, which was under the Seventh Service Command at Omaha, was sent to survey the possibilities. Although he gave approval to the plan, he said it needed the approval of the commanding officer at Omaha, Nebraska.

A public hearing was held at the Olivia Court House on Monday, August 23, 1943. Area residents were assured that POWs would not interfere with local labor. They were told that 100 Italian prisoners accompanied by thirty-five guards would arrive in two weeks' time, and would be housed in tents near the old tile plant in Olivia.

In attendance at the meeting were members of the Renville County Farm Labor committee. There was no opposition to the proposal, so final approval was given. Wages were set at fifty cents an hour to be paid to the government for transportation, food, clothing, and other camp expenses. The captives themselves received eighty cents a day for a ten-hour work day plus an extra $3.00 per month.

By September 2, the Olivia site was in shape and had been fenced. Water was piped in, and lights were installed. Arriving by special train from Camp Clark were prisoners captured in North Africa. All had been enlisted men in the Italian army. Their average age was twenty-one, but one man was fifty-five years old. Only a few spoke English, making it necessary for Army officers and company officials to communicate with the leader through two soldier-interpreters of Italian descent.

Forty regular Army men accompanied the captives. The guards worked in shifts with constant surveillance of the POWS in camp and in the cornfields where they worked during the day.

Speaking at the Kiwanis Club meeting on Tuesday, September 7, 1943, Captain G.B. Howell and Lieutenant J.W. Kent, who supervised the POWs, reported that the prisoners were an "orderly and happy group of Italians." "Sometimes," said Howell, "there is a snatch of song as the men stop for a cigarette." At first, they rolled their own, but, as they earned money, they bought ready-mades at the camp canteen. All had volunteered to work in the corn fields. One POW said it was better to work than to loaf in Camp Clark, Missouri. Said Howell, "Their leaders are responsible for their organization. They do their own cooking supervised by an Army mess sergeant."

Seven prisoners were assigned as cooks and KPs to deal with the food and supplies procured from Fort Snelling. The Italian POWs consumed more spaghetti and less meat than the American Army guards, and they were more interested in a big soup bone than in a steak. To show their appreciation for the opportunity to work in Olivia, the POWs prepared an Italian dinner for the Kiwanis Club of the city.

For leisure time, a recreation room was made available in the basement of the armory. Soccer and volley ball were available. With Sundays off, the internees could attend religious services. A local priest said mass at the prison camp.

Howell and Kent noted that there were a number of talented artists and musicians among the prisoners. They also said that all donations for the comfort or entertainment of the American soldiers with them had to have the approval of the commanding officer. As usual, contact with the POWs was not permitted, but the officers said they hoped to make the Olivia camp a model one.

A report in the *Olivia Times Journal* on September 16 noted that when Captain Howell informed the Italians that Italy had surrendered to the Allies on September 8, most of them seemed pleased. A few hung their heads, but most cheered. Formerly, the captives saluted in Fascist fashion, but about the middle of September, they asked Captain Howell to teach them the American salute.

At the end of the season, the POWs returned to Camp Clark, Missouri, leaving on October 25, 1943. Great satisfaction in their work was expressed by George Sawin, local company manager of Rogers Seed Company. "They did a good job. They were fast in picking," he said, complimenting the POWs.

Chapter 6

Prisoner of War Base Camp, Algona, Iowa

THE NORTHERNMOST BASE CAMP in the VII Service Command was located about three miles northwest of Algona, Koseuth County, Iowa, on U.S. Highways 18 and 169. The Algona base camp was activated at the end of December 1943, and the first prisoners of war, a contingent of 501 Germans, were received on April 6, 1944. The Algona site was chosen because it was far from war-related industries and was close to forests and farms where laborers were needed.

Originally under the command of Colonel Church, the camp was placed under the command of Lieutenant Colonel Arthur T. Lobdell in June 1944. Formerly at Clarinda, Lobdell was said by Howard Hong to be "a high type of man, desirous of developing a high type of camp." Major Louis C. Hutton was Lobdell's executive officer with Captain Clifford M. Jenner as special services officer.

The 287-acre POW camp was located on almost-level land surrounded by rolling farm country with occasional tree-lined creeks running through it. Buildings were constructed in December 1943 by the utility branch of the engineering department and were maintained by that unit. As the camp developed, streets and sidewalks were graveled and graded, and one hundred trees furnished by the U.S. Forestry Service were planted around the camp.

A standard chain link double fence with a barbed-wire over-hang surrounded the well-lighted stockade. Depressions caused by drainage ditches under the fences, seen as possible points of escape, were barred. Head counts of POWs were made twice a day with the prisoners assembled in the yard. Formation was held until every man was accounted for, including those on duty or in the infirmary, a 150-bed hospital, fully equipped and staffed to serve the base and the branch camps.

Security actually was not a problem. Of the more than 10,000 prisoners who went through Algona and its branch camps, none walked away from job sites. Lieutenant Colonel Lobdell said that if a German soldier gave his word, he would keep it. Many times the POWs were allowed to go to their jobs unescort-ed as long as they gave their word they would not try to escape.

Designed as a base camp, Algona had a capacity of thirty-two officers and 3,000 enlisted men. The purpose of the base camp was to relocate POWs into branch camps where the captives would be put to work. As a result, the population of Algona gen-erally was less than 200 POWs. A report by Howard Hong dated July 18, 1944, listed only 180 prisoners in the compound. Among them were non-commissioned officers, six medical officers and two clergymen. The rest had been relocated to branch camps. As of August 1, 1944, eight POW branch camps had been estab-lished with the following populations: Moorhead—159, Remer—236, Owatonna—117, Deer River—157, New Ulm—163, Fari-bault—140, St. Charles—120, and Ortonville—113.

Exactly one year later the report on branch camps listed the following numbers: Owatonna—207, Fairmount—512, Deer River—165, New Ulm—317, Bena—145, St. Charles—259, Fari-bault—423, Montgomery—643, Wells—313, Ortonville—111, Moorhead—85, and Remer—0.

Special efforts were made to complete the POWs' 201 per-sonnel files. Weekly officers' meetings were held, with semi-week-ly meetings with non-coms. The purpose of these assemblages was to discuss problems and study the regulations of the Geneva Convention and any POW circulars released.

Algona was responsible for providing rations and supplies to two of the POW branch camps in Minnesota—Fairmont and

Wells. Rations and supplies for other Minnesota camps were provided by Fort Snelling.

In the Algona camp, religious services were conducted by Lutheran and Catholic clergymen from the area. An American chaplain, Captain Traugott K. Herbener, arrived at the post in late summer 1944.

Activities in the base camp were difficult to arrange because of the movement of prisoners to branch camps. Development of schools was a particular challenge. Finally a standard number of minimum courses was developed so that the work would be the same in every location. As men transferred from one branch camp to another, they could continue their studies. Howard Hong suggested that a director-registrar be selected at Algona to supervise the coordination of educational programs. Later, correspondence course work was developed for the branches through the University of Minnesota. The German Reich Ministry of Education offered full high school and university credit for courses taken in the United States by POWs.

Shortly after the camp opened, a male chorus was formed with the original purpose to celebrate a marriage by proxy (the wedding ceremony was performed without the bride). With the exodus of POWs to branch camps, the chorus was dissembled.

Many of the Germans were interested in arts and crafts. Wood carving and painting were pursued, with carpentry tools, power tools, and painting materials made available through the International YMCA, International Red Cross, National Catholic Welfare Conference, Lutheran Committee for POWs and World Students. A German architect designed the interiors of the dayrooms and the furniture for them, and the POWs carried out the plans, building the pieces needed.

As far as sports were concerned, there was little difficulty in turning the flat Iowa prairie into football and soccer fields.

Every base camp, of course, had its contingent of American officers. The following American officers were posted at Algona as of September 1944:

Headquarters:

Lt. Col. Arthur Lobdell, camp commander
Major Louis C. Hutton, executive officer

Capt. Raymond K. Glattfelder, post adjutant and personnel
Capt. Traugott K. Herbener, chaplain
Capt. Wilbur J. Lynge, post quartermaster
Capt. Earl L. Milstgead, compound commander
Capt. Donald R. Montgomery, post engineer
Capt. George C. Myers, labor relations
Capt. Gunnar A. Norgaard, assistant executive
1st Lt. Robert T. Cumback, headquarters detachment
    commander
1st Lt. Murray Greenbaum, post exchange officer
1st Lt. John H. Jernigan, post ordnance officer
2nd Lt. Richard P. Baughman, finance officer
2nd Lt. Arthur E. Perry, post judge advocate.

Station Hospital:
Major William L. Yetter, post surgeon
Capt. Joseph O. Mona, chief of dental services
Capt. James B. Lavender, post veterinarian
1st Lt. Harold Sofron, chief of medical services
1st Lt. Julia M. Urbanski, chief nurse
1st Lt. Donald R. Zito, dental officer
2nd Lt Jacob Greenberg, chief of laboratory services
2nd Lt. John S. Devick, adjutant, station hospital.

American enlisted men at the camp in September 1944, numbered 227, with 204 in Headquarters Detachment and twenty-three in the Medical Detachment. The ranking POW spokesman was T/Sgt. Walter Bauer.

Efforts were made to "Americanize" the Axis prisoners. By letting them listen to the radio, read books and magazines, it was hoped that some of them would absorb an idea of democracy and would work toward that end in Germany in the post-war period.

Some of the POWs apparently learned too well one phase of Americanism. The inmates in the Algona camp staged a one-day strike. They refused to work on Adolph Hitler's birthday, April 20, 1944.

Chapter 7

Camp No. 1,
Moorhead

OPPOSITION IN MAY 1944 TO THE PROPOSED HOUSING of 150 German prisoners of war within the city limits of Moorhead, Minnesota, gave rise to the possibility that the project would be abandoned. Paul Horn, who with Henry Peterson had contracted to employ the men from June 1 to November 15, planned to house the POWs in a large barn owned by Clifford Warner near Twelfth Avenue and Elm Street

German prisoners of war posed for a photograph on the Henry Peterson Farm near Moorhead, Minnesota. Although it was against the policy of the Geneva Conference to allow photographing of POWs, a number were taken. (Courtesy of Henry Peterson Farm Papers, Northwest Minnesota Historical Center, Moorhead, Minnesota)

South near the Red River. Protests from nearby residents were numerous. Still the site was the only one approved by Army inspectors who had surveyed the locale. A public hearing held in the spring favored the use of prisoners to relieve the labor shortage.

Plans were carried out and on Sunday, May 28, an advance detail of forty Germans arrived with guards from Algona. Second Lieutenant Richard M. Blair was commanding officer. T/Sgt. Eric O. Brasch, second in command, spoke German. The POWs spent Sunday night in tents on the Horn farm south of Moorhead before they were moved to a warehouse at Twenty-first Street and Fourth Avenue North owned by the Moorhead Onion Growers Warehouse Association. The barracks building was dim but cool.

The balance of prisoners, 120 men, arrived Wednesday, May 31, on the Northern Pacific Railroad. These captives had seen service in North Africa, Sicily, and Italy. They, too, were marched to the Onion Growers warehouse. Moorhead residents were assured that the POWs would be under military guard at all times.

Using materials provided by the government, the inmates did all the work necessary to renovate the camp, including the installation of an eight-foot wire fence around the sixty-foot by 170-foot warehouse. A guard tower was planned but never built. The men improved the buildings and even installed a fish pond.

Horn and Peterson owned truck farms of nearly 7,000 combined acres in the Red River Valley. Taken by truck to the farms, the POWs worked six days a week, planting, hoeing, and picking vegetables. Their output was only sixty-five percent of what immigrant labor could do. The contractors paid forty cents an hour to the government. Of that, thirty cents went toward housing and feeding the POWs, giving the government a small profit from the use of prisoner labor. The government, in turn, gave coupons to the POWs worth ten cents an hour redeemable at the camp canteen.

According to Horn and Peterson, the POWs were friendly and nice people. They received humane treatment from Blair and the farm contractors, so there was no trouble. Peterson even sent flowers and fruit to sick POWs hospitalized in St. Ansgar Hospital. He took them to the theater twice and gave them "bier und cigarettes," which was within regulations.

German prisoners of war on the Henry Peterson Farm near Moorhead, Minnesota. The POWs worked six days a week, planting, hoeing, and picking vegetables. (Courtesy of Henry Peterson Farm Papers, Northwestern Minnesota Historical Center, Moorhead, Minnesota)

Florence Drury, bookkeeper on the Peterson farm in 1944, had a different opinion of the prisoners. She said the POWs were Nazi-types, who strutted and goosestepped. A few broke a pump with a sledge hammer. After a sit-down strike in September, fourteen prisoners spent time in the Clay County jail.

On Sundays, Blair took the captives swimming at Buffalo River or to the Benedict Gravel Pit southeast of Moorhead. The city closed Twenty-first Street after business hours and on Sundays because local people cruised by the camp to see the POWs. This was contrary to the Geneva accord, said the *Fargo Forum* and *Daily Tribune*.

An article in the *Forum* dated June 6, 1944, was titled "Curb Travel to Prisoner Camp."

"Because the presence of a prisoner of war camp at Moorhead's eastern outskirts has been attracting hundreds of sightseers and causing a traffic jam, the city council Monday authorized Lieutenant Richard Blair to block the street leading past the camp when necessary.

"Lieutenant Blair told the council that more than 500 automobiles traveled the road Sunday, making it necessary to station one of the soldier guards as a traffic cop. The officer also pointed out that one of the strictest army regulations requires that prisoners of war are not to be subjected to the public gaze. Not only automobile traffic, but groups of young girls also created something of a problem, he said.

"Twenty-First Street, leading from U.S. 10 to the Paul Horn Onion Warehouse past the camp where 150 German prisoners are quartered will be blocked Sunday afternoons and on weekdays after working hours to all except essential travel, the lieutenant said."

Howard Hong visited Moorhead Camp No. 1 early in August. He found no books and arranged for a library to be sent from Algona. The only music available was furnished by one accordion player. Some sports were provided, and arts and crafts materials were ordered for the camp, as well as a wood carving kit and embroidery materials. Weekly church services were conducted by local Catholic and Lutheran pastors.

German prisoners of war at work on the Henry Peterson barn. POWs could be required to work for the benefit of their captors. They could not, however, be employed in any war-related work or in unhealthy, dangerous or degrading labor. (Courtesty of Henry Peterson Farm Papers, Northwestern Minnesota Historical Center, Moorhead, Minnesota)

Lieutenant Blair was returned to Algona after the September report that found the camp dirty and poorly policed. He was replaced by Lieutenant B.C. Davis, who opened Twenty-first Street. Davis reinforced the tenets of the Geneva Convention by limiting conversations between the contractors and prisoners. He barred gifts between civilians and POWs and forbade them from entering businesses or riding in the cabs of trucks.

Late in 1944, it became the policy of the United States to Americanize the POWs and to expose them to democracy in the hope of creating a democratic post-war Germany. With that in mind, prisoners were encouraged to study English, watch movies, and read books geared along these lines.

When the harvest was completed in November, the POWs were returned to Algona. A smaller group returned to Moorhead in July 1945 with Sergeant Roy Schultz as second in command. The new regulations were still in force. Some $1,100 in improvements had been made to the onion warehouse. The kitchen and dining room were separated from the sleeping quarters, and the prisoners continued to do their own cooking. Schultz said they were pretty good cooks. The wire fence was removed. The captives elected their own leader who spoke to the authorities on their behalf.

At a hearing held July 19, it was reported that there was more trouble with the guards than with the prisoners. Peterson called the guards "hillbillies." That situation would be remedied when returning veterans who had families or relatives in the Red River Valley area were assigned as guards.

Citizens of Moorhead were upset when they learned the POWs received meat three times a week, whereas it was rationed to civilians. It was pointed out that the Geneva agreement stated that prisoners should be fed the same as American servicemen. As shortages grew worse in 1945, more severe food restrictions were enforced on the home front. In compliance, meat, fat, and sugar were cut from the POWs diet, and replaced with starches.

The POWs returned to Algona in fall after the vegetable harvest was complete and were repatriated to Germany the following year. One former prisoner wrote that he was in the United States for two-and-a-half years. He said, "It was a good school for me. Not only were the Americans good workers, but good fellows."

Chapter 8

Camp No. 2, Fairmont

PLUMBING EXTENSIONS AND OTHER ALTERATIONS were being made at the fair grounds in Fairmont, Minnesota, on Thursday, May 2, 1944, in anticipation of turning it into a prisoner of war camp. According to the *Fairmont Daily Sentinel* of that date, final arrangements had not yet been made. However, it was expected that POWs would be used as laborers in the canning factory. The fair board said that the contract would run until September, so it was expected that the fair, held before that, would run as usual. The fair grounds at Blue Earth was being readied for the same purpose.

Two days later, Fairmont Canning Company announced that it had contracted for approximately 1,100 foreign workers for the 1944 crop harvest. That number included 325 German prisoners from Algona. The POWs were to be field workers and harvesters. None would work in the plants. Prisoners were to be paid the same rate per hour as civilians.

Prisoners would not come in contact with civilians except in rare cases where a foreman directed their work, and guards were to be with the POWs at all times. The captives' camp would be surrounded with barbed-wire, and the stockade would be lighted at night. POWs were to be treated under the rules of the Geneva Conference.

It was necessary to build a kitchen, bath house, and other facilities. United States soldiers who accompanied the prisoners were quartered in a separate area adjacent to the internment camp.

Arrival of the German POWs was expected about June 15 when the first pea crop was ready for harvest. An advance detail would assist in construction of the camp.

This was the information carried in the Fairmont newspaper prior to the arrival of the captives.

The first contingent of some thirty to forty Nazis arrived at 12:15 P.M., Sunday, June 4, 1944, guarded by infantrymen under the command of Second Lieutenant Jake Orff. They were housed in the 4-H building on the fair grounds where they did their own cooking. Civilians were warned that they were not permitted in the camp area. Women particularly were forbidden around the installation. An added warning was included: "Some of the prisoners of war have been in the Army for two years, and haven't seen a woman in that time."

Three days later, two more truckloads of prisoners brought the total to about 100. Civilians lined the highway near the fairgrounds to watch their arrival. They waved and tried to talk to the internees. The prisoners thumbed through their German/English dictionaries to interpret what was said. They seemed very happy, said one reporter. A few POWs who spoke English said they would come back there to live. "Fairmont is very pretty. It looks like a park," they were quoted as saying.

Good food, a good place to sleep, and good medical care were given to the prisoners. The Reverend A.M. Beck, and the Reverend D.H. Zemke, who spoke German, started conducting worship services for the men. A priest from Algona base camp offered Catholic services.

The commanding officer of Branch Camp No. 2 at Fairmont was Captain Joseph G. Gaitskill, Corps of Military Police. A former judge of district court in Gerard, Kansas, Gaitskill was a veteran of World War I. He had fifteen assistants including guards. Along with other branches, Camp No. 2 received its rations from the base camp at Algona. Gaitskill, as did other commanding officers, warned the civilians not to try to take pictures of the prisoners. "If you do, you face confiscation of the camera, and/or removal of the film, and maybe a call from the FBI." One camera had already been taken by the guards.

The *Fairmont Sentinel* of June 15 recorded that locals tried to talk through the fence to the POWs. Some smuggled edibles to them. "Giddy females trying to carry on a flirtation with the Nazis are due for summary discipline," was the admonition. Two girls who crawled through the fence to the internees were thrown out.

In September, some 130 POWs were on the job at the Fairmont Canning Company. An item in the September 5 newspaper stated that production in the cannery had dropped, and it couldn't handle the crop for lack of manpower. Appeal was made to the POW camp at Algona. Within twenty-four hours forty Germans, guards, and equipage were moved to Fairmont where POWs would help with the canning for the next four or five weeks. The men worked in shifts at the factory with some thirty POWs attending to routine work at the camp. Their "stalag" was in the old inn and cottages at Interlaken Park, which had been closed for years. A ten-foot woven wire fence enclosed the quarters "to protect the prisoners from predatory females and other wild animals" stated the *Fairmont Daily Sentinel.* Deputy Sheriff Henry Striemer was on duty at the camp to prevent civilian interference.

It was noted that the Germans appeared healthy and well-nourished, and it seemed doubtful that they would try to escape. Two of the Nazi NCOs spoke English. They asked if they could have lard instead of butter as a bread spread, as they carried sandwiches to the canning factory for their lunch, and preferred lard.

Well-fed, well-muscled Germans help relieve the manpower shortage in Martin County as they work in the pea fields and pea viners. They put in twelve-hour days seven days a week and pitched an average of 3,500 pounds of pea vines an hour per man. (Courtesy of the *Fairmont Daily Sentinel*)

Captain Gaitskill herded the whole contingent to the beach at Amber Lake one September day for an early morning dip even though it was somewhat cold. The POWs seemed to relish it.

This notice was posted in the canning factory: "POWs working in this plant are enemies of the United States. Accordingly, it is a high crime against our government for any civilian employee to communicate, consort with, give aid or comfort to any of these men. It is forbidden to converse with them unnecessarily or to pass written messages to them, or to give or receive any gifts from them." Penalties were severe for people who violated the rules. They could be charged with treason. At the factory, a wire enclosure surrounded the machines at which the prisoners worked.

Captain Gaitskill spoke to the Fairmont Rotary early in October, discussing the terms of the Geneva Conference. The treaty signed by more than forty nations outlined how POWs should be treated—"with extreme care," said Gaitskill. He spoke again at the November meeting of the College Women's Club, detailing the program for prisoners of war in the United States. He urged Americans to hold their anger in check even though they thought POWs were being treated too well. The actions were guided by the Geneva Conference, and the Germans were well-schooled in the Articles. They knew what they could demand.

By March 1945, 140 prisoners were billeted in barracks formerly occupied by Mexican workers. Three of the buildings contained sleeping quarters; one had a kitchen and dining hall, and one was equipped with a latrine, showers and laundry. The administration offices shared space with the infirmary and canteen, which contained all the articles authorized by the War Department.

Eighty prisoners worked in the meat factory, while others labored in agriculture. Some were engaged in carp seining for eastern markets. According to German spokesman Theodore Lier, the POWs didn't like assembly line work, especially the preparation of chickens. Twenty men suffered an infection of their hands from the chickens. While health among the captives was generally good, there were some cases of grippe.

The prisoner details replaced civilians at night, and the trip to and from the factory took three hours. In their eight-hour shifts, the POWs accomplished about ninety-five per cent of what the civilians did. Because of the inconvenience of travel time to work, and the damp terrain, commanding officer Gaitskill concurred that Fairmont was the least-favored of all branch posts.

In their leisure time, internees participated in wood carving, reading, handball, ping pong, and volley ball. Movies were shown bi-weekly. A small POW orchestra consisting of piano, violin, accordion, guitar and drum, gave concerts.

As the war continued into the spring of 1945, civilian rations became more limited. As a result, the prisoners of war were put on a new diet that eliminated most fresh meats, canned fruits, canned vegetables, and butter. Fresh meats were restricted to hearts, liver, kidneys, brains, tripe, and neck bones.

On learning of Germany's unconditional surrender, the German POWs in Fairmont prison camp took the news without much show of emotion. So many things had happened, it was said to be hard to put a finger on the reasons for their dejection. Rations had been reduced. There was no more beer. Tailor-made cigarettes were not available, although they still had paper and loose tobacco. Candy, cookies, and crackers were unavailable. The "Hitler salute" was ruled out and replaced with the standard German military salute.

The internees had their own radios and heard the news leading up to the surrender. They learned that 1,391 out of 3,102 prisoners in Camp Devon, Massachussets, signed a petition asking their former comrades in arms to surrender. "There is a future, but it must be without Hitler," they insisted. "Continued war means total destruction of the homeland, and bleeding to death of the people," continued the petition.

Then came news of Benito Mussolini's death, followed by news of Adolph Hitler's death. This at first was doubted by the POWs. With the official announcement of the surrender, the prisoners became concerned about when they would be permitted to go home or would be turned loose.

Summer 1945, found prisoners still at work in the Fairmont area. Several hundred assisted in harvesting Martin County's bumper crop of peas. At the Art Loring viner two miles east of Imogne, the Germans worked two shifts. The first was from 6:00

A.M. until 5:00 P.M. The second remained on duty until the day's allotted acreage was in. Said Mr. Loring, "So far as work is concerned the German prisoners are the best help we've had at this viner. They almost work too hard. I have to keep slowing them up as it takes steady pitching to keep the viner operating at maximum efficiency."

The POWs pitched an average of 3,500 pounds of pea vines per hour for twelve hours. That figured out to about 42,000 pounds of peas in one work day. The meager food allowance of the prison camp was increased for the pea harvesting crews. Other prisoners, not employed in such strenuous work received less food.

A sample of a day's menu:

Breakfast: oatmeal, black coffee, bread.

Lunch: potatoes, cabbage, tea.

Dinner: hash. Meat about once a week.

The camp at Fairmont was closed on December 14, 1945.

The Fairmont prisoner of war camp as pictured on December 12, 1945. Property of the Fairmont Canning Company, the camp was dismantled two days later. The German prisoners of war, with United States soldiers guarding them, and all military equipment were removed. (Courtesy of the *Fairmont Daily Sentinel*)

Chapter 9

Camp No. 3, Remer

IT WAS WITH A SENSE OF RELIEF THAT FORESTRY OFFICIALS learned that German POWs were to be used in the effort to cut a record pulpwood and chemical wood from the Chippewa National Forest.

On the last day of January 1944, an American officer, First Lieutenant Jacob A. Yockey and eighteen Army guards escorted thirty-seven German privates to a former CCC Camp in the Chippewa Forest two miles northeast of Remer in Cass County. A few days later, the camp at Bena was opened. In April, 131 POWs arrived at Cut Foot Sioux. At first, all were under the jurisdiction of the Concordia, Kansas base camp. In June, they were transferred to the supervision of the new Algona, Iowa, headquarters.

At the Remer camp, buildings were of frame construction painted green with white trim. Many improvements were made by the prisoners. As an example, the eight sleeping barracks were partitioned by the POWs with birch wood to afford privacy. Policing and upkeep of the grounds by the internees was outstanding. The mess hall seated 250 men, and kitchens were rated excellent. Cooking for both the Americans and Germans was done by the prisoners, with food at the POWs' tables the same as on the camp commander's table. One difference was noted in the War Manpower Commission Report of February 25, 1944: "We ate the regular chow served the POWs which I recommended, with the exception of the potatoes. They have a way all their own of rolling the mixture of boiled and raw potatoes together in a sort of dumpling. Not too bad if eaten with plenty of strong gravy."

A small infirmary was adequately supplied. The 201 personnel files of the captives were kept up to date. A day room, recreation hall, canteen, library with German books, and ping pong tables were located in a building twenty feet by seventy feet. The POWs engaged in wood carving and painting. Those interested in music made guitars and zithers. Phonograph records were sent from Algona.

The camp had a five-acre athletic field. Tennis courts were constructed, as well as a fussball court for a German game similar to volleyball. Boxing gloves, ice skates, baseball equipment and soccer balls were provided. A room twenty feet by forty feet served as a chapel and as a class room for courses in music, math, and philosophy at the university level; in English, forestry, math, German, and literature at high school level. A priest from St. John's College conducted services. The men built a birch altar and pulpit for the chapel.

The camp was surrounded by a single barbed wire. No guard towers were erected. Lighting was termed "inadequate." Security was maintained by two guards patrolling the area during the day, three at night. Prisoners were allowed out of the stockade on business only. The recreation field could be used from 6:00 to 8:30 P.M. The POWs could swim in a nearby lake, but before going to the beach they had to report to an American officer to have a guard assigned as escort.

By February 25, there were 247 POWs at the camp. The count on July 3, 1944, listed three officers, thirty NCOs, and 215 enlisted men. The work details traveled thirty miles into the woods by truck, and they labored from 6:30 A.M. to 6:30 P.M. A hot meal was served at noon. Because the site was so isolated, only minimum guards were needed. One report noted that there was an absence of guards with rifles. Either they were concealed or the POWs were given full privilege of the honor system.

The prisoners cut four-fifths of a cord of wood a day. Some 160 to 180 POWs cut trees, sawed them, pealed the bark, and piled the timber on skids. The rest of the internees were engaged in maintaining the camp, cooking, and other housekeeping chores.

The captives were not supermen. The average height was five foot, nine inches. They were described as having somewhat swarthy complexions, and they were devoid of military bearing.

Many pets were allowed on the grounds, ranging from a snake to a small fawn, which the POWs fed with a bottle.

Morale at the camp was exceptionally high. The POWs used the Nazi salute to the United States Army officers. It was returned with the U.S. Army regulation salute. Many internees spoke broken English. They said that northern Minnesota was "schust like Germany."

Chapter 10

Camp No. 4, Bena

THE CAMP AT BENA WAS ONE OF THE FIRST OPENED in Minnesota, having been activated January 31, 1944. Men were shipped from the Concordia, Kansas, base camp to the Chippewa National Forest in Minnesota. In June 1944, the commanding officer was Lieutenant Aretzki. First Lieutenant Vincent B. Hughes was listed in a July report as commanding officer. The compliment of prisoners consisted of four officers, eighteen NCOs, and 197 enlisted men. By September of that year, Captain Kenneth F. McClintic was commanding officer. During the height of its operations, the Bena camp contained one American officer, fourteen American enlisted men, one prisoner of war officer, and up to 160 prisoner of war enlisted men. Rations were delivered from Fort Snelling.

The Timber Production War Project of the United States Forest Service compiled a pamphlet for use by the guards and contractors. It contained "100 sentences and 50 common words to help you instruct Germans in how to work safely and more easily in the woods." Directions for use of the pamphlet carried the sentence, "If they don't understand you, show them the German words."

Samples from the booklet include the following:

Attention	Achtung	ahkTOONG
Get on the truck	Auf den Wagon steigen	auf den VAHgen STYgen
Always yell "timber"	Rufe "achtung" wenn	ROOFa AHKtoong
	Baum fallt.	VEN BAUM FELT.
Watch out for	Achte auf fallende	AHKTa AUF
falling branches	Aeste	FAHLenda ESSta

Contractors at Bena were Goss and Richard Lumber Company, and Melvin Mettler and Andrew Giffan, dealers in lumber. The POWs labored at reforestation and cleaning up the slash harvesting of trees. This was primarily seasonal work. During the winter, the POWs engaged in cutting and peeling pulp wood, cutting tie bolts, skidding and cutting logs, and swamping. They were paid $3.00 per day.

The camp was located 300 yards behind a tourist camp in Chippewa National Forest, almost on the shores of a lake. The facilities included barracks, canteen, day room, theater, chapel, a swimming beach area on the lake, soccer field, and workshop. A Benedictine monk from St. Cloud conducted Catholic services. A POW pastor from Cut Foot Sioux camp held services every fortnight.

The POWs made fifteen boats from scrap lumber. These were used within limits on the lake. The Fish and Game Commissioner said there were legal complications regarding issuing fishing licenses to the prisoners, so none were available. At one point 100 POWs were seen boating on the lake adjacent to the camp. Perhaps because they were not under guard at the time, civilians engaged them in conversation in spite of rules against such contact.

An active school was instituted with instructors coming from the ranks of the POWs. Classes were held in French, English, chemistry, history, and mathematics. Individual music lessons were given to fifteen men. More than 200 books were available in the library. Some prisoners engaged in painting and wood carving.

According to a report dated May 20, 1944, there were 219 men at the Bena Branch camp. Contract workers numbered 115. Of them sixty POWs were assigned to Goss and Richmond, twenty-five to Andrew T. Giffen, and thirty to Melvin Mettler.

Kitchen forces in camp were POWs and consisted of a sergeant in charge, six cooks, a baker, six KPs, and a fireman.

The camp at Whitewater State Park near St. Charles was nestled among hills. Inset is United States Army Captain J.E. Elson, commanding officer of the camp. (*Courtesy of the Rochester Post Bulletin*)

Overhead workers numbered ninety-three. They were engaged in sawing, fencing, repairing the road, wood cutting, policing, driving wood to the barracks, unloading wood in the camp, and digging a victory garden. They served as drivers, firemen, clerks, typist, carpenters, orderlies, painters, post exchange clerks, and mechanics. One man was a medic, one a barber, and one a tool sharpener.

On the date of the report, there were three officers and one doctor, one man sick in the barracks and paid, four men sick and not paid, and two men unemployed.

In June 1944, a newly-formed orchestra consisted of accordion, trombone, five violins, two guitars, base drum, two mandolins, and piano. The recreation hall, complete with stage, was from the former CCC camp. An outdoor bandstand was constructed by the internees.

According to a report by YMCA field secretary Howard Hong, prisoners had been transferred from Camp Concordia to Algona, then to Bena. Field Liaison Officer Captain Lyle T. Dawson wrote that Bena was reactivated September 23, 1944, by transfer of POWs from Ortonville. At the end of 1944, it was expected that the camp at Bena, along with those at Remer and Cut Foot Sioux (Deer River) would continue through the winter.

Chapter 11

Camp No. 5, Owatonna

BROUGHT FROM THE GERMAN INTERNMENT CAMP at Concordia, Kansas, a contingent of thirty-five prisoners of war arrived at Owatonna, a town of 6,000 inhabitants, on March 25, 1944. They prepared the grounds at the Cashman Nurseries Farm north of Owatonna to accommodate approximately 100 POWs. Eight barracks each held eight men. Other men slept in the administrative building in which the mess hall and kitchen were located. A recreation hall was created in a building that had a shower in the basement.

The prisoners were in the custody of twenty officers and enlisted men with First Lieutenant Basil W. Poynter, Jr., as commanding officer. When the full complement arrived, the number of guards was increased to twenty-eight.

The Steele County labor shortage was met partially by the Germans who were to supplement the work of Owatonnans, not replace them. The POWs were employed at Cashman Nurseries, Inc. and Owatonna Nurseries from April 1 to June 8. After that they transferred to the Owatonna Canning Company, putting up peas and asparagus.

Although many of the prisoners spoke English, Friedrich Hektor was spokesman for the POWs. Many were skilled in trades and in farming, and all were volunteers, saying it was much better to be working than to be idle in camp.

The POWs were not permitted to attend church in town, but chaplain service was allowed with local clergy presiding. Medical services, adequate food, and recreation were provided. The German doctor was allowed to work only as a member of the sanitary committee. Serious medical cases were treated by a doctor from Owatonna. Food was termed good and plentiful, with rations and supplies provided by Fort Snelling. A cold meal and hot coffee were served at noon to POWs working in the canning factory.

When Howard Hong, YMCA field secretary, visited the camp on June 26, he found that no classes were being held. A lawyer gave a history lecture once a week. The camp had two small phonographs and forty-two records, so music programs and theater productions were held along with poetry readings. The theater manager in Owatonna held special showings of movies on Sunday mornings. Hong left a violin, a clarinet, and music for the camp. POWs participated in fist ball and ping pong. Since travel to and from their work stations was on their own time, the POWs sometimes didn't get back to camp until 8:00 P.M. and, therefore, had little time for recreation.

In his report of August 9, Hong noted that prisoners had arrived from the camp at Bena, which was closed temporarily. They were under contract to the cannery, but between pea and corn canning they were subcontracted to farmers for shocking and threshing. Seven men were mechanics in a garage.

By November, Hong saw that an English class had been established using the YMCA book *Kleine Englische Sprachlehre.* Classes were held in commercial arithmetic and correspondence. The medical officer gave lectures on biology. Readings of literary masterpieces were given, and musical activities were prominent because the prison doctor was a pianist. A trio made up of piano, violin, and cello was practicing and performing. A chorus had been formed.

The three-storied nursery building burned down in January 1945. It was rebuilt, with the new structure providing better quarters for the inmates. Day room and class quarters were much improved over accommodations before the fire.

By the time the camp was one year old, its programs were well developed. Religious services were conducted by Methodist pastor Reinecke and Lutheran pastor Bonhof who gave lectures on Minnesota history. The camp priest served mass at branches in Owatonna, Montgomery, and Faribault. Occasional literary lectures and readings were also given by the priest. A six-member orchestra was formed with the German doctor as orchestra leader.

The prisoner laborers continued in nursery and creamery work.

A report by a Mr. Zehnder made to the U.S. Army Provost Marshal on March 10, 1945, stated that Friedrich Hektor was spokesman for the camp. There were a medical officer and fifty-seven German NCOs and privates. One complaint was that the POW doctor was not permitted to practice. He only worked as a member of the sanitary team. It was suggested that an exchange of doctors be made with the main camp to allow prisoners who were doctors to follow their profession.

During an inspection conducted on June 24, 1945, by Provost Marshal General Major D.L. Schweiger and Captain C.E. Tremper a specific recommendation was made. The POWs were ordered to remove a picture of Adolph Hitler from the mess hall.

As in all the branch camps, POWs followed the course of the war on the radio. Americans worked hard to show the benefits of democracy and freedom of the press. Prisoners were assured that the news they heard was not propaganda because they were allowed to listen to reports of race riots and strikes then occurring in the United States. That convinced them that the news releases of German military reversals were true.

Chapter 12

Camp No. 6,
Deer River (Cut Foot Sioux)

"EXCEPT FOR THE ABSENCE OF A BAND, the occasion might have been a Fourth of July celebration from the crowd of curious sight-seers who greeted their arrival."

That was the description of the appearance in Deer River of the German Prisoners of War. The *Deer River News* reported that the first POWs reached the town about 4:00 P.M. on Wednesday, April 5, 1944, by special train from Camp Concordia in Kansas. These were men assigned to the logging camps. About twenty vehicles met the train. The 150 or so POWs were taken by truck to former CCC Camp 707 located near Squaw Lake. This became Deer River Branch Camp No. 6 with Second Lieutenant Kenneth A. Braun in command. After dinner at a local cafe, the platoon of American soldiers who had escorted the POWs boarded the train and were on their way back to Kansas.

(According to notes in the Itasca County Historical Society, a total of about 1,275 prisoners arrived early in February 1944 to work in branch camps at Remer, Cut Foot Sioux, and Bena.)

The previous Monday, a score of U.S. soldiers had been taken to the camp to ready it for the prisoners.

Observers of that unique parade noted that the prisoners were young, some just fifteen or sixteen years of age. They seemed jolly and happy. One truck had a dog in it. Several POWs had musical instruments in their luggage.

In 1944, many of the German prisoners were young, some only fifteen or sixteen years of age. These men shown in the fields on the Henry Peterson farm near Moodhead are typical. Although issued clothing by the United States Army, many of the POWs wore parts of their own uniforms. (Courtesy of the Henry Peterson Farm Papers, Northwest Minnesota Historical Center, Moorhead, Minnesota)

Contracts for the prisoners had been negotiated through Headquarters of Minnesota Branch Camps at Remer. The Deer River contractors were Max Logging Company, Toivo Hovi, Victor Terho, and Jake Reigel.

The internees were put to work cutting and peeling pulp wood, cutting tie bolts, cutting and skidding logs with horses, and swamping. Army trucks were used to haul the captives to and from camp, and a lieutenant who had been a forester in Germany accompanied the POWs and supervised their work.

Three weeks after the camp opened, about twenty-five American soldiers and guards stationed at Cut Foot Sioux (Deer River) and Bena enjoyed the hospitality of the Deer River Junior Association of Commerce. A party was held for them with the purpose of getting acquainted and giving the visitors an evening of social contact with local men. All enjoyed cards, visiting, and lunch.

In spite of that conviviality, a few months later there was a run-in between the locals and the "visitors." E.R. Starkweather, deputy director of the Division of Game and Fish, was checking out reports of confrontations between game wardens and the soldiers. There were incidents of GIs shooting ducks and other game and of fishing illegally, a practice "seriously frowned on by people of this section." The soldiers were reported to their commanding officer, who promised that firm action would be taken to prevent any recurrence of such conduct. Several prisoners of war were put on bread and water rations in the Itasca County jail. Their crime—fishing out of season without a license.

Captain P.L. Schwieger made a report to the Provost Marshal on July 3, 1944. He said that the commanding officer of the base camp had recently replaced all American personnel at side camps "with the most inefficient personnel—had literally 'shanghaied' them to Northern Minnesota." He continued that there had been no unfriendly incidents between guards and prisoners, but there was too much fraternization. At Deer River, Schwieger observed, both POW officers and American officers shared quarters outside the compound. He recommended that the POWs be moved inside the fenced area.

On that date, Captain Harry G. Bracken was in charge of the Deer River site. Prisoners included four officers, nineteen NCOs, and 108 enlisted personnel.

Starkweather checked on the possibility of obtaining fishing licenses for the prisoners, but no provisions were made for such permits. The captives were not entitled to hunt or fish, even under non-resident licenses.

Cut Foot Sioux was closed at the end of the season. Late in January 1945, prisoners were moved from the Remer CCC camp to a CCC camp at Day Lake. These POWs had worked in the woods year round and had finished cutting in the Remer area. Timber operations continued through the year in Sucker Bay and Third River areas.

After a few months, Army guards didn't bother to accompany internees to the work sites. Some POWs were allowed to go shopping in Deer River with guards. Others even were taken into town on Saturday nights to have a drink.

In winter, POWs often stopped at the Forest Service station to get warm, and, in turn, the Forest Service had its snowplow repaired by the prisoners. Foresters found the prisoners to be well-disciplined.

All was not well in town, however. A war of words took place between the locals and the soldiers. A headline in the *Deer River News* on Thursday, May 3, 1945, announced "Lax Administration of the Prisoner Camp causes Indignation." It seems that Game Warden Bob Greig returned to camp with two POWs whom he picked up for fishing out of season and without licenses. Commanding Officer Lieutenant W.P. Schweidenberg didn't want the incident reported in the newspapers.

The game warden replied that he would not take orders from the Army. The commanding officer threatened that the warden would have to answer to the Army if the report got out.

People in the community were incensed at the freedom given the prisoners. Warden Greig and a local businessman found two prisoners fishing on a lake about a mile from camp. They were unattended and unguarded. Area residents were particularly irate because a home-town boy had returned after being held prisoner by the Germans. Locals knew that American prisoners in Europe were not allowed to roam all over the countryside. A further complaint was that German POWs were sleek and well-fed. They were getting cocky and quite arrogant. Sentiment in the community ran high. Telegrams were sent to congressmen and to Army officials about the way the POW camp was run.

At the end of the month, Lieutenant Colonel A.T. Lobdell, Commanding Officer of Algona, Iowa, base camp conducted a tour of inspection and looked into the complaints. He was accompanied by First Lieutenant J. Jernigan of motor maintenance at Algona and escorted by Captain F.K. McClintic, commanding officer of both Bena and Cut Foot Sioux camps. On finishing the tour, Lobdell stated, "It is possible a number of prisoners will be taken from the camp in summer and transferred to an agricultural region."

The war with Germany had ended on May 7, 1945. When asked how long the prisoners would remain in the Deer River area, Lobdell replied that for each American man returned or discharged, a prisoner would be released and returned to his homeland. The operation could take some time, because of the need for transportation.

The POWs were still at Deer River in June 1945. YMCA field secretary Howard Hong reported that the men at that branch were paid $3.30 per day, compared to $3.00 at Bena. He asked the Provost Marshal to check into this discrepancy.

Hong reported that the camp had a recreation field, volley ball field, full-size baseball field, recreation hall, stage, and piano. The mess hall was also used for classes and lectures. Fort Snelling provided rations and supplies to the camp.

Chapter 13

Camp No. 7,
New Ulm

HAVING A GERMAN POWS CAMP NEAR NEW ULM was a different situation from that in other locations. The city had been founded a century earlier by immigrants from Germany, and much of the population still spoke German. Many families still had relatives in Germany, giving them a sympathetic connection with the prisoners. Older people particularly felt sorry for them.

The first notice of the arrival of POWs in the New Ulm area was carried in the *Brown County Journal* on May 16, 1944. Lieutenant George O. Gilead, labor relations officer from the prisoner of war camp at Algona, Iowa, visited New Ulm to inspect the proposed camp site. He indicated that Brown County would get POWs, speculating that the first group would arrive about June 1.

"Excitement reigned along Broadway for a short time this morning as the first detachment of Nazi war prisoners rolled into the city to prepare the old Transient Camp on the banks of Cottonwood lake for the 150 prisoners that will be encamped there to help with the work at the Sleepy Eye canning plant."

Such was the notice in the *Brown County Journal* on June 4, 1944. The article continued, "It was a happy crew of prisoners that filled the two army trucks. They smoked and conversed among themselves while watching the number of onlookers who were just as curious to get a look at them. They were a crew of young men, apparently happy to be out of the war, and the first thing they spotted along the street was a "beer" sign which one prisoner apparently read to the rest."

Bob Steinboch was in high school in New Ulm when the captives arrived. "I thought they would look different than Americans, but they didn't," he said.

"A few girls walking along Broadway caused a rousing cheer from the trucks as they rolled past on their way to camp," continued the newspaper article.

The convoy arrived in the city about 10:00 A.M. Led by an officer's car and patrolled by a company of soldiers, the troop cavalcade rolled into the city, and the officers were given directions to the camp. W.A. Nelson, area director of the War Manpower Commission said that thirty men under the directorship of Lieutenant Dietrich were scheduled to begin cleanup of the camp, with the remainder of the crew to arrive later.

Tentative contracts had been written in May 1944, with Fairmont Canning, Faribault Canning, Lakeside Canning of Faribault, Lakeside Packing Corporation in Plainview, and California Packing Company in Sleepy Eye to use POWs headquartered in New Ulm.

Early in June, Nelson had asked for tools to be used in putting the camp in Flandreau State Park in order. Axes, spades, shovels, hammers, crowbars, and similar items were needed, but the Army didn't provide tools. Sleepy Eye Canning Company, which would employ some of the prisoners, pledged to make good on any tools broken, damaged, or lost. A few days later, Nelson said that three wheelbarrows were still needed. Community response to provide tools had been excellent.

Located in a forested valley some 200 miles north of the base camp at Algona, the New Ulm site was one of the most attractive camps in the upper Mississippi region. Originally it was a transient relief camp erected in 1934 for unemployed men during the Depression. Later it became a CCC camp. That was discontinued in January 1942.

The Cottonwood River had been dammed to form a small lake about 100 yards from the log-sided cabins in the trees—a barracks containing kitchen and mess hall, seven "hauser," a recreation hall with fireplace and library, and a shower building. The day room was enhanced through construction by the prisoners of peasant-style furniture. An infirmary could accommodate five patients. The camp was surrounded with a low, barbed-wire fence. Guards at New Ulm were part of the 410th Military Police Escort Guard Company with headquarters in Arkansas. The rent for the site was fifty dollars per week.

The Brown County prisoners were described as vigorous, and ranged in age from eighteen to twenty-five years. They worked hard felling trees and cleaning up the camp.

In July, the POWs received thirty-two gallons of paint for the outside of the camp buildings, and they repaired a root cellar on the site. The next month they started building a football field. The well-stocked camp canteen carried for sale all articles on the official Geneva Conference list. Food for the New Ulm camp came from Fort Snelling, and prisoners of war were permitted to swim in a certain part of Cottonwood lake.

German twin brothers Hans and Werner were captured together and interned together at New Ulm. (Courtesy of the Brown County Historical Society, New Ulm, Minnesota)

The "spokesman for the group was named Tietz, twenty-five years old, friendly and cooperative," the *Journal* wrote. "The men were fixing up a clubhouse for leisure hours. They would like German language books. Donations may be left at the *Daily Journal* offices."

Although the captives were heavily guarded and civilians were warned that contact with them was not acceptable, the *New Ulm Daily Journal* of June 9, 1944, reported two contacts made with the public.

The Reverend E.J. Markhausen of Emanuel Lutheran Church of Courtland offered to give services in German. His offer was accepted. "I will treat them as I would like my son treated if he were captured," he said. Lutheran services were held on Sundays and Wednesdays. Catholic services were conducted on Sundays. The POWs built an altar for use by the chaplains.

Reverend F. Sells of St. Paul, who worked with thousands of POWs through the Missouri Synod, said "Only fifteen percent of them are Nazis—Godless, atheistic, arrogant, practically hopeless and beyond redemption. These are mostly officers. 'Germans,' mostly privates, were men who were pressed into service."

An unplanned contact occurred when Herman Schaper, a *Journal* paper carrier, and a friend were on a hiking trip in the hills near the POWs camp. The boys had stopped to fix a meal when two prisoners approached.

"You're frying eggs wrong," said one prisoner and showed them how to do it. The internee spoke in German. Herman was fluent in the language, so the two carried on a friendly chat. The prisoners were interested in news of the Normandy invasion. At the conclusion to their chance encounter, one POW gave Schaper the silver Nazi corporal chevron from his uniform.

Prisoners interned in New Ulm found a slice of home in the German-speaking enclave of New Ulm. Women sent baskets of food to the camp, and young girls flirted with the POWs. Those working in the canneries bought them ice cream and beer on their breaks.

Because New Ulm residents didn't understand the rules governing the treatment of prisoners, Lieutenant Arthur S. Roberts, commanding officer of Camp No. 7, wrote an explanation of the Geneva Convention of July 1929, which was printed in the local newspaper. He reminded people that nations must provide ample food, comfortable housing, good sanitation, and sufficient recreation.

The visit of Howard Hong on July 24, 1944, found many musicians but no instruments. Musicians could play piano, Hawaiian guitar, zither, accordion, and mandolin. A male chorus was being formed. A local Little German Band played concerts once in a while. The POWs had room only for fist ball, but when equipment was made available, they played tennis and soccer. Hong announced a painting and carving contest to be held among the branch camps. There was plenty of interest, he said, but the men needed materials.

The main body of 150 or so POWs arrived June 18, 1944. The prisoners worked mostly in the cannery. Some seventy-five Mexicans did the outside work.

Charles Crouch of Sleepy Eye, supervisor at the cannery, said the Nazis who had been with Field Marshal Rommel in Africa were arrogant and thought they were supermen. One former member of Rommel's Afrika Corps had to be sent back to Algona because of the problems he caused by insisting the other POWs salute him.

There was feeling among the prisoners against the SS (Secret Service) types. At Nordling Canning Company in Cokato, two SS members had to be segregated. According to employee August Anderson, there was fear that the hard-core Nazis would be injured by the other prisoners. Most of the POWs were more compliant and happy to be here. They had fun, said Crouch.

The POWs harvested and processed vegetables for the California Packing Corporation in Brown and Faribault Counties, and the Del Monte Canning Company near Sleepy Eye.

Richard Arbes, cook room supervisor at the Sleepy Eye Cannery, had twenty-two to twenty-eight POWs working in the cook shop and in canning. They ranged in age from sixteen to fifty-five years old. The young ones were the last ones drafted into the German Army. They said they were picked up off the streets with no training, fitted with uniforms and sent to the front. Arbes said the Germans were well fed before and after their twelve-hour shifts in the canning factory, but they had only coffee and bread during work hours. He brought sandwiches and milk for them. Break times were congenial, with the prisoners talking about the Old Country.

The first day at the cannery, guards were all over the plant, even on the roof. After a couple of days, however, the guards disappeared. When it was time for the buses to take the POWs back to camp, the guards appeared. Sometimes the prisoners had to go and look for them because "We can't go home without the guards."

Herbert Richter was one of several former POWs who returned to the United States and lived in Kenosha, Wisconsin, for thirty-five years. On Memorial Day 1985, an interview with Richter was taped in which he described his vivid memories of the prisoner of war camp at New Ulm. A native of Schweidnitz, Germany, he had joined the German Air Force at age nineteen and became a radio operator. He was shot down over Allied territory. Sent to the Cottonwood River branch camp, he first worked in the German kitchen washing dishes. When a cook was needed for the American guards, Richter volunteered. He met people from New Ulm—the ice man, the baker, and the butcher because he went to the butcher shop several times a week.

Richter recalled Sunday afternoon band concerts given by former members of the German Air Force in front of the recreation hall in the camp. People from New Ulm came to listen and sang along in German along with the music.

POWs on local farms fared the best of all. They were fed meat and potatoes, vegetables, and desserts at the family table and occasionally given beer. One of the farmers, Carl Ramberg said, "We weren't supposed to feed them, but you couldn't expect them to work on an empty stomach. We weren't supposed to visit with them, either, which was rather cruel."

Betty Lou Bastien, who lived on a farm where the captives worked, said they were nice. "You could laugh and have fun with them." Francis Beranek recalled that her parents, who farmed in the Lafayette area, hired prisoners to help in harvesting grain, shucking and threshing. The farmer had to pick up the POWs at the camp, and every weekend return them to the camp. She said the internees were good workers and were happy to stay at their farm during the week.

There were a few reports of swastikas being painted on barns, but the captives offered no real threat. In fact, they were so manageable that often the guards left for the day.

When the season at the canneries was over, the POWs in the pea and corn pack were released from their employment. It was decided that the prisoners would stay at the camp until winter. They were employed at the American Art Stone Company of the New Ulm Brick and Tile yards and in the Ochs Brick and Tile plant in Springfield about fifty miles from New Ulm.

Larry Ochs, son of the brick yard owner, had been in Europe at the time his family employed POWs labor. He said, "Without the prisoners, the business would have closed down. They took on just about every job in the setting and machine room, sorting bricks for color, and shipping."

POWs at the Ochs Brick and Tile Company in Springfield, Minnesota, located about fifty miles from the New Ulm camp. (Courtesy of the Brown County Historical Society of New Ulm, Minnesota)

In November 1944, the camp was made ready for winter. The next month, the guard house burned. The cause of the fire was a leaky oil burner. The POWs built a new one.

Not all the people in New Ulm were happy to have the German soldiers in the area. Joyce Aufderheide wanted no part of the POWs. She heard that women from town who still had memories of the old country and had ties through relatives there brought pies and cakes to the camp and slipped them over the fence. "I don't know if that's true," she said in a 1985 interview. "I certainly didn't. They made me angry. My husband was over there. I was bitter."

63

German prisoners of war at the American Artstone Company in New Ulm, Minnesota, in 1945. (Courtesy of the Brown County Historical Society, New Ulm, Minnesota)

Joyce was married to Jack Aufderheide, whose grandfather had contracted to have prisoners work at his brickyard. Joyce saw quite a lot of the POWs, whom she said were mostly arrogant. Jack Aufderheide returned to New Ulm from an internment camp in Europe to find his enemies working in the family business, enjoying a good living, being treated like kings. He went to work two or three weeks after he got home, and he got rid of the POWs. "I resented them and didn't want anything to do with them."

The spring of 1945 once again found 143 German prisoners at the Cottonwood camp, mostly NCOs and privates. The prison doctor was a captain in the medical corps, and the spokesman was T/Sgt. Tietz. Again the POWs worked for the canneries and on farms.

Farmer Daniel Dietz said the guards had to shoo away the young women of New Ulm who walked along the river to visit the Germans.

Iris Mathiowetz of Red Wing recalled that her father hired prisoners to help with the harvest. She said they were surprised and happy to land in New Ulm, a German-speaking community that practiced its German heritage. Her parents were very good to the POWs because they were so happy to have their help. Although farmers weren't supposed to feed the captives, her mother served them treats. At first Iris was afraid to have the prisoners so close because she thought they were Nazis, but she grew to like them.

At the end of the war, food became as poor for prisoners as it did for civilians. Herbert Richter, POW cook for the captain and guards, said the menus went from pork chops and steaks one day to potatoes and herring the next.

As death camps were uncovered in Germany, New Ulm soldiers saw what the Nazis had done in camps at Dachau and Buchenwalt. They wrote home of what they had seen. Feelings toward the Germans prisoners of war changed. Sympathy was gone. The POWs were again the enemy.

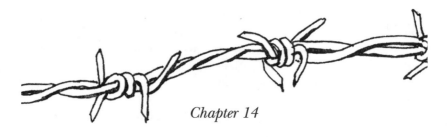

Chapter 14

Camp No. 8, Montgomery

CONTRACTS WERE SIGNED ON MAY 27, 1944, with Minnesota Valley Canning Company to employ 350 prisoners of war. The Germans, working within a twenty-five-mile radius of Montgomery would be used in pea vining from June 20 through July 25. From August 10 to September 25 they would be corn snapping.

The first contingent of thirty German prisoners of war arrived on Saturday, June 10, 1944, at Camp No. 8 at Montgomery, Minnesota. This was a work battalion that traveled in trucks from Algona to prepare a camp near the cannery. The POWs were accompanied by a lieutenant and soldiers to serve as guards. Buildings, which in former years had been occupied by Mexican workers, were prepared to house the internees, and additional buildings were put up. The entire tract was fenced and two guard towers erected. Lieutenant Comeback and a corps of thirty-two soldiers were housed outside of the POW camp. With a count of approximately 600 internees, Montgomery was one of the larger camps in Minnesota.

The balance of the prisoners—288 of them—arrived by special train on Friday, June 23, to work at the Minnesota Valley Canning Company. Lieutenant Arthur S. Roberts was in charge of the POWs and their guards. The POWs marched from the railroad siding to the camp on the south end of the cannery property where they would be interned.

According to Blanche Zellmer, who worked in the cannery, some prisoners were housed for a time in a government hemp plant. "Hemp was grown here for making rope for the Armed Forces. The plant was closed sometime in '45, and some POWs were housed there," she said.

The nearby city of Austin, Minnesota, was subject to some propagandizing by the Axis internees. As the special train passed through town, it stopped briefly on the Milwaukee rail track near the Brownsdale Avenue crossing. Richard King, a Milwaukee Road yard clerk and his brother Warren were standing near the train after Richard had finished icing the cars, and he saw a blond POW about in the middle of the train open a window and drop some papers to the ground.

After the train left, King retrieved five sheets. Hand-printed in crayon and pencil, the papers had swastikas on the back. King took the sheets to the *Austin Daily Herald*. The editor turned them over to FBI officers in St. Paul. Because it had no jurisdiction over the POWs, the FBI forwarded them to the War Department.

One of the hand-drawn leaflets read: "Americans. Quit the war! You gein (sic) nothing but blood, sweat, and tears!"

A sixth leaflet turned up on June 22, 1944. It was found by James Borris of the North American Can Company under the seal of a boxcar on the tracks near the point at which the POW train had stopped. This leaflet was not hand-made but had been printed from wood type. The propaganda was turned over to County Sheriff Arnold Eckhardt. It read, "American Mother! Where is your son? He is lying dead on the fields of France. What is he fighting for? You don't know."

The editor of the *Austin Herald* telephoned Duane Dewel, editor of the *Kossuth County Advance* published in Algona, Iowa. Dewel confirmed that, because similar leaflets had been found at Algona, the prisoners had been searched before they boarded the train at the Algona camp. In spite of this, a number of leaflets had been scattered en route from Algona to Montgomery. Dewel also offered the information that, during the search, guards had found a hand-drawn map of the United States on one POW. He added that generally the prisoners processed through Algona were in two groups—the young who were still Nazi-inspired, and older men who were more conservative and not addicted to Hitler.

According to M.M. Malone, cannery supervisor at Montgomery, the Germans would be used in fields and at vining stations. They would work in groups of ten to fifteen and labor eight hours a day. The cannery paid sixty cents an hour for services.

The Nazis were between twenty and twenty-four years of age, all captured in the North African campaign. They had their own cooks, medical men, and interpreters. All supplies for the Montgomery branch came from Fort Snelling.

A big attraction at the Montgomery community park one Sunday followed the local ball game. A soccer game was played between the German prisoners from Faribault and a team picked from the Montgomery camp. Montgomery POWs won six to four.

To assist in the corn pack, sixty more prisoners arrived from Algona by truck in mid-August. These men had been captured in Normandy.

Remembering the time she worked in the cannery alongside the prisoners, Blanche Zellmer said, "We weren't allowed to speak with them. Of course, most everyine that worked near them sneaked in a word here and there."

Censorship was very strict during the war, Zellmer recalled, so newspapers didn't publish anything about the POWs. "I know I myself tried to take some pictures there which were confiscated," she said.

A report dated September 16, 1944, listed Captain Clyde W. Snider as commanding officer of the camp with fifteen guards and one medic at the site.

In two months' time, the corn pack was finished. On October 9, the Germans broke camp. Some left by truck for Algona. Others were sent to Faribault, and still more went to northern Minnesota to the lumber camps.

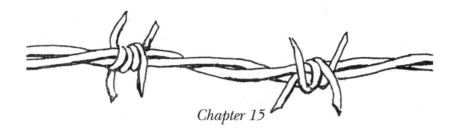

Chapter 15

Camp No. 9
Faribault

IN RESPONSE TO AN ANTICIPATED LABOR SHORTAGE, the Minnesota Canners Association in January 1944, requested that the War Manpower Commission make available 3,000 prisoners of war for field and factory operations. In March, Army officers inspected possible housing facilities for prisoners at Faribault, Minnesota. An advance unit of German prisoners arrived in Owatonna on March 23 to prepare a camp there. In April, it was suggested that the St. James Episcopal Boys School in Faribault could house prisoners. The school's board of directors rejected the idea, claiming that the facilities were inadequate.

In May, the Faribault Canning Company took out permits to build four barracks buildings in which to house POWs. The camp was located right next to the cannery. The company also contracted with the prisoner of war camp in Algona, Iowa, for 200 prisoners to work at pea vining from June 20 to July 25 and corn snapping from August 10 to September 25. Between seasons, the POWs could work on grain harvest for local farmers.

At a meeting of the Faribault city council on May 23, a delegation from the Packers Local Union appeared to protest any importation of German prisoners. The mayor responded that the city had no authority to reject or approve the project.

A small contingent of prisoners arrived in Faribault on June 20. Eventually there were more than 200 prisoners housed at the

Barracks built in 1944 by the Faribault Canning Company for prisoners of war. The barracks were razed in April 1990. (Courtesy of the *Faribault Daily News*)

canning company, working in two shifts at the factory. The first captives had been shipped from Concordia, Kansas, to Bena, and then to Faribault. Canteen funds were lost en route, so the POWs were not able to purchase supplies.

By August 9, 1944, the camp was under the supervision of First Lieutenant Basil W. Poynter, Jr., who found the red tape of official channels difficult. No recreation supplies had been received from Algona. Still the POWs had some magazines for leisure reading, and there was a ping-pong table. There were also some implements for wood carving. A musician was pleased with the guitar available to him. The POWs were allowed to swim in the "dubious" Cannon River, according to YMCA field representative Howard Hong. At the end of his visit, he left sports balls and carving tools at the camp.

Ruth Thibodeau remembered working at the canning company when the prisoners were there. In an interview with Pauline Schreiber of the *Faribault Daily News* in April 1990, she said, "You absolutely weren't allowed to talk to them. I was nineteen at the time, and the prisoners were somewhere between twenty to twenty-five years old. I worked on the cutter, and they worked some-where else in the plant.

"From what I can remember, they were more like trustees than prisoners. They were supervised, but the guards didn't have guns or anything like that. They [the POWs] had to stay in their designated area."

Martin A. Paschke was supervisor of the canning company at that time. Interviewed by Schreiber, he said, "They were the best workers we had because they liked it over here. Many of them got to like it so much they wanted to stay after the war. They worked regular shifts like anyone else. They had their meals in the bar-racks and stayed there during their free time."

Paschke recalled that one group included an artist. "He could really paint some good pictures." Company officials had no problems with the POWs.

At the end of the canning season, some of the prisoners win-tered in Bena and Owatonna. The rest were returned to the base compound at Algona. The camp at Faribault closed for the sea-son on November 20, 1944.

Once again in April 1945, POWs were sent to Faribault. The camp was reopened because of the many requests for farm help. The first arrivals constructed new barracks. According to an excerpt from the 1945 Annual Report of Rice County, Minnesota, internees first were put to work in Andrews Nursery. The follow-ing month they worked at the Faribault Canning Company. "Without prisoner help," stated the report, "it is very likely that the canning company would not have been able to pack their peas or corn."

Between the two packs, the POWs again were of great assis-tance in the harvesting operations of farmers in both Rice and Dakota counties. POWs were engaged in silo filling and shocking corn with the cooperation of the Faribault Canning Company. Each day orders for help were placed at the office of the employ-ment service office. The agent went to the canning company and checked out the number of prisoners requested by individual farmers.

Because of the dangers of an eat-work-sleep existence, Hong helped establish creative programs. General education

Between the packs at canning companies, POWs were of great assistance in harvesting crops. Germans pose during the carrot harvest on the John Reynen Farm near Hollandale in the fall of 1945. Reynen is the man with the bucket. Seated at the right is John's son Al with his wife, Doris, standing behind him. (Photo courtesy of Al and Doris Reynen)

was offered for free time with reprint texts available from the YMCA. The only musical instruments available were twelve mouth organs until other instruments later were provided by the Red Cross.

The report of Field Secretary Hong on August 9, 1945, noted that the commanding officer of the camp was Sgt. Milligan. By then a school had been organized, but more books were needed for the classes. Hong brought dictionaries. The POWs had formed an orchestra, and held concerts using phonographs and records provided by the YMCA.

An accident involving POWs was reported in the *Albert Lea Evening Tribune.* On Monday evening, September 4, 1945, twenty-seven internees were bruised and shaken up when a school bus used to haul them to and from Dakota County farms overturned between Faribault and Northfield. According to the operator of the bus, Hastings farmer H.W. Schaar, a tie rod broke, the bus went out of control and careened up a bank where it hit a tree and overturned. The POWs climbed out through front and back windows. They were returned to the POW camp for medical attention. One of the group suffered a broken collar bone.

Rice County received 11,195.5 man hours of work from the POWs during the months of August, September, and October, 1945. This figure did not include the Germans used by Andrews Nursery Company; rather it was work furnished to individual farmers.

The prisoner of war camp was quickly disbanded after the end of the war, according to geneologist Arnold A. Madow of the Rice County Historical Society. The POWs were returned to Algona for repatriation. In later years, the Faribault Canning Company used the barracks as housing for contracted foreign laborers from the West Indies. Said Madow, in April 1990 the barracks were demolished to make way for an expansion of Faribault Foods, Inc., the former Faribault Canning Company.

Chapter 16

Camp No. 10
St. Charles

A SMALL CLUSTER OF BUILDINGS NESTLED among the high bluffs at Whitewater State Park six miles north of St. Charles, Minnesota, served as temporary Branch Camp No. 10 for prisoners of war during the summers of 1944 and 1945. This was a former CCC

POWs eating their evening meal in the camp dining room at the Whitewater camp near St. Charles, Minnesota. Cooking in the camps was done by POWs themselves. The prisoner second from the left at the middle table was only sixteen years old and was a member of a labor battalion when captured. (Courtesy of the *Rochester Post Bulletin*)

camp located south of the golf course of the park and had earlier housed Works Progress Administration workers. On the site were nine barracks, one shower and toilet building, a black smith shop, mess hall, office, and an officers' barracks. An office and medical unit were operated by the German prisoners. Tables and chairs set up on the lawns in the compound were kept painted by the POWs. The commanding officer of the camp was United States Army Captain Jack I. Elson. American Army personnel were quartered in barracks outside the prisoner compound.

The buildings were remodeled to house up to 200 POWs. Around the camp was erected a ten-foot fence topped with three strands of barbed wire. High intensity flood lights were installed at each corner of the fence and at appropriate locations around the camp. The Whitewater Park supervisor said the POW camp would in no way interfere with the program of recreation at the park. The prisoners' presence would not even be noticeable.

The main assignment of the captives was to ease the labor shortage at Lakeside Canning Company in Plainview by assisting with the pea and sweet corn packs.

"Encamped in one of the nation's beauty spots were 100 POWs from Algona," according to the Thursday, June 29, 1944, issue of the *St. Charles Press.* Guarded by United States soldiers from Fort Snelling, the prisoners had a POW interpreter "who spoke English in a gutteral manner" but was very well understood. Ages of the prisoners ranged from fifteen to twenty-five years. One reporter noted that the Nazis were stoical and self-centered. They felt that the people of the United States were misinformed as to the real Nazi program of civilizing the entire world.

Infrequently the internees were marched from the camp to the town of Elba. En route, they would pick out "their" farms, confident that the time was coming when Hitler would win the war and they would be able to live in the United States. At first they jeered at reports of mounting losses by the Nazis and held firm in their loyalty to their homeland. As new inmates were brought from the Algona camp, the POWs learned of German setbacks on the battlefield, and they began to recognize the inevitability of defeat for the Third Reich. After the May 1945 Allied victory in Europe, the POWs worried about their families and whether or not their homes and farms would be intact upon their return to Germany.

As of July 25, 1944, when jobs at the canneries were completed, prisoners were made available in groups of ten to aid in harvesting, shocking and threshing grain. The minimum work day was five hours; the maximum was eight. Contracting farmers picked up the men at the CCC camp in the morning and returned them in the evening. A guard, who was not paid by the farmers, accompanied each group to its assignment. Prisoner help was available within a twenty-mile radius of the camp. Contracts could be let for only three months. On occasion, when other work was not forthcoming, prisoners were detailed to work at the state park.

Typical of the farm employers was Ralph Hildebrand who said he hired several of the POWs. After a morning of hard work, the Germans sat down to a dinner of dry bread and water. Feeling sorry for the men Hildebrand invited the POWs into his house for a warm meal. Although this was against the policy of the camp, many farmers fed the prisoners, believing that they needed good food in order to work as hard as they did.

Farmer Ray Speltz of Lewiston employed a prisoner named Conrad Strumph during the harvest season. Speltz remembered, "I used to pick up Conrad at the park and take him home each day. We used him for threshing and shocking chores. He was treated like any other hired man, being fed, since we didn't expect help to work without eating."

(Although regulations specified that the captives were to be used in groups of ten, it was permitted for several farmers to pool their requests for farm labor, enabling one pod of ten men to work on a number of farms.)

In autumn 1944, the POWS returned from the St. Charles branch to the Algona base camp. Again in April 1945, German prisoners were brought to Whitewater State Park to relieve the labor shortage. They worked on farms until the beginning of the pea harvest. At that time more POWs were brought to Whitewater. Some of these had been employed in the woods in northern Minnesota.

That year, in addition to being employed at the Lakeside Canning Company in Plainview, Germans were put to work on the receiving dock of the Reid-Murdoch Canning Company plant in Rochester. This marked the first time enemy prisoners had been hired in that city. The POWs ranged in age from sixteen to fifty years. The number used at the dock depended on the number needed each day.

On farms the men could be put to work fencing, painting, manure hauling and performing field work. Many were able to operate tractors and other machinery. Prisoners were allowed to be away from camp for twelve hours, working for ten hours. The camp provided breakfast and supper, with supplies and rations sent from Fort Snelling. Prisoners carried their lunch to work.

The first year the prisoners were at St. Charles, hundreds of people drove to Whitewater State Park on Sundays and evenings to gawk and hope for a chance to see a "real Nazi." By the summer of 1945, the public lost interest, and the camp drew little attention.

Farmers and contractors reported that the work done by the POWS was more than satisfactory. Some of the men were farmers; others were students, carpenters and businessmen. The Germans were quick to learn and adaptable to most jobs given them. Most men appreciated being out of the war. Most were well-disciplined and obeyed orders implicitly. When trouble did break out, the guilty parties were put on a diet of bread and water. Infractions of regulations meant withdrawal of the few privileges they enjoyed. In some cases it resulted in incarceration in the municipal jail.

Pay given to the internees went into a trust fund, or into coupons which could be redeemed for merchandise at the camp canteen. If not transferred or spent, the funds reverted to the United States government. The canteen at Whitewater carried shaving equipment and soap. There were no cigarettes or cigars. Occasionally, pipes were made available.

One favor was a dole of two ounces of tobacco each week. Many POWs managed to fashion crude cigarette-rolling machines. A number of the POWs enjoyed hobbies. Tools and blueprints for such things as model ships, musical instruments and paints could be purchased with their funds, ordered through the base camp at Algona, Iowa.

Some passed their time listening to 78-rpm records. The Germans did not seem to enjoy playing cards. Two wiled away the evenings working on a detailed replica of the *Mayflower*. The highly-intricate and accurate model of the ship had doors which opened, guns which retracted on their mounts, and a rudder which turned. The *Rochester Post Bulletin* offered a generalization, stating "The swaggering, insolent, died-in-the-wool Nazis, the troublemakers, have pretty well been weeded out."

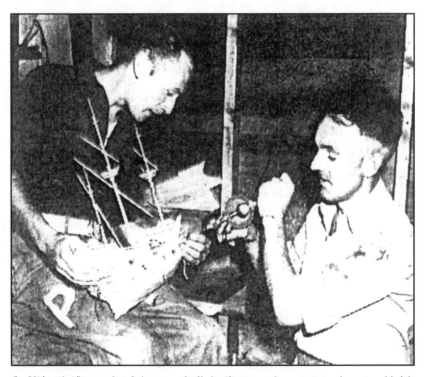

Two POWs at the Whitewater State Park camp near St. Charles, Minnesota, work on an intricate and accurate model of the *Mayflower*. The man on the right was a professional carpenter near Breslau, Germany. The man on the left was a truck driver and made model ships as a hobby. (Courtesy of the *Rochester Post Bulletin*)

Commanding Officer Jack I. Elson said that there were no demonstrations at the branch camp on V-E day, only tenseness among the prisoners. An officer in the U.S. Army infantry, he had been in command of prisoner of war guard units in the Seventh

Service Command since September. He said the Germans did not air their political views, at least not in front of their American captors. There was never any mention of Hitler. When German prisoners were first brought to the United States, officers and enlisted men were kept at the same camps, but were segregated as it was discovered that there was always trouble when the two were mixed, said Elson.

He noted that there had been no escapes or attempted escapes from the Whitewater camp. As the guards pointed out, "The POWs realize there is no place for them to go if they did escape, and they are better off here."

An article in the July 17, 1945, *Bulletin* reviewed life at Whitewater. "A library at the camp allows prisoners to purchase books with money they earn. The books, printed in German, are sent out from Algona, a certain number to each camp. American newspapers are available, and from radios in the barracks, they [the prisoners] may listen to any programs they choose." Radios [no short wave, however], newspapers, and phonographs with mostly classical records were on hand for POW use. Classes in English were conducted with seventeen prisoners attending on a voluntary basis. Only one German among the captives understood and spoke English fluently. He was a highly-educated man who spent his spare time painting pictures. "Some of the best I've ever seen," according to Captain Elson.

The article noted that the diet was monotonous, with a lot of soup. Mutton was the only whole meat the POWs received. Otherwise ox tails, salt pork, kidneys, hearts, livers, and powdered eggs made up the main part of the menu. Prisoners were cooks and bakers for the entire compound, as well as for the detachment of Americans.

Eight or nine of the POWs organized a band and practiced almost every night for their Sunday concerts. Much of the music was classical, but they also played a lot of American tunes. A soccer field inside the camp and a football field across the road from camp were available. The POWs planted a garden.

A visit in June 1945 to the St. Charles camp by Howard Hong, YMCA prisoners' aide elicited a report that the site was satisfactory for an all-winter camp. There was a possibility the men might be put to work in a large laundry in Rochester.

That was not to be. By October 11, evacuation of internees from Whitewater had been completed. The POWS marched to the Chicago Northwestern Railroad station in St. Charles and boarded special coaches. Most were going to Crookston, Minnesota. Twenty were kept at the camp to take down the wire enclosure and clean up the site. In a few days, they too were gone. That marked the end of a program which had caused considerable excitement a year earlier when the United States was still at war with Germany.

Ten of the buildings of the old CCC camp were destroyed by a tornado in the summer of 1953. The remaining buildings were torn down to make room for the campground at Whitewater State Park.

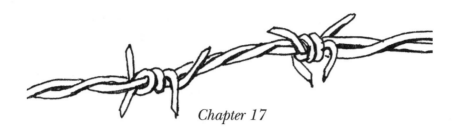

Chapter 17

Camp No. 11, Ortonville

During the harvest season in 1944, Camp No. 11 was opened at Ortonville. On July 6, the *Ortonville Independent* recorded that prisoners were at work readying the barracks at the Big Stone Canning Company. Some 112 or more POWs aided in the fields and as laborers in the warehouse during the corn canning season.

Commanding officer of the camp was Captain Clifford M. Jenner with T/5 Ernest S. Williams as assistant. Williams also acted as medical officer. Headquarters for the United States Army officers was the former Miller home adjoining the POW barracks.

Quarters erected at the camp included kitchen, mess hall, bath house with showers, sleeping quarters and athletic field, all electrically lighted all night long. Fencing enclosing the camp was mainly to keep the curious from mingling or talking with the POWs. Rigid restrictions were enforced. No talking to prisoners was allowed and definitely no photographs of them were to be taken.

The Germans worked in crews of ten to twenty, shocking grain, and manning two shifts at the cannery.

The *Independent* reminded residents that the captives were not felons. They were prisoners of war. Many were doctors, lawyers, and men who once ranked high in German civilian life. "Curiosity-bent folks are requested not to evidence undue interest or concern on the POWs arrival or during their stay," the article concluded.

Internees were made available for farm work throughout the area. Ten worked at the Degreep farm near Big Stone City. Another group went to Graceville. A third went to the Hugo Ebert farm east of Ortonville. Because sixty of the more than 100 prisoners were farmers, the local contractors were very satisfied with their labor.

Sergeant Mattord, second in command in August, said the Germans shocked 8,000 acres of grain up to the end of July. They gave 430 man days of labor.

Chapter 18

Camp No. 12, Howard Lake

A story in its Thursday, August 3, 1944, edition of the *Howard Lake Herald* revealed that the Northland Canning Company of Cokato had made arrangements with the Wright County Commissioners for use of the county fairgrounds to house German prisoners of war. The mess hall and dining room would be located in the grandstand. The lower part of the grandstand was to be the canteen. The agricultural exhibit building in the southwest of the grounds would be barracks. Approximately fifty men, mostly young boys and old men taken prisoner in Normandy, would be under the control of Military Police. The POWs would be in the area for about sixty days picking sweet corn for the cannery. They were to be paid between fifty and eighty cents a day.

Although the Provost Marshal's report of August 8, 1944, listed twenty-eight prisoners at the "branch" at Cokato, none ever were quartered in that city. They were interned at Howard Lake and transported to the Cokato cannery by Army truck.

The first group, twenty-six in number, arrived from Algona the following week. Shortly thereafter the total reached about 100. Sgt. Carl Testhammer, a veteran of the American campaign in North Africa, was in charge with seven other Military Police and guards in his command. Prisoners O.P. Jungclaus and H.W. Vogel served as interpreters. The Germans had been taken prisoner in Cherbourg. Because of their age, either seventeen or fifty years of age, they had been in labor battalions, not in the front lines, when captured.

E.T. Jacobson, personnel superintendent at the cannery took an active part in directing the POWs, using the German language he had learned in college. The internees set up showers in the 4-H poultry exhibit hall, and put bunks in the agriculture building. The POWs seemed willing to adjust to captivity. Some were raking leaves and digging in the dirt to ready the camp for habitation. One of the prisoners, a master plumber, installed the showers.

Clothing was informal. Some of the men wore shorts; some went shirtless. Some were hatless; some wore caps or straw hats. "PW" was stenciled on their shirts, pants, and caps.

An article in the *Cokato Enterprise* noted that the prisoners were shorter in stature than the average American. All were strong, tanned, and in excellent condition. Few were young. These were the "expendables" left at Cherbourg when the Nazi troops pulled out.

One forty-year-old captive had a fifty-seven-year-old brother fighting in France. The captive had been a chauffeur for German officers at Cherbourg. He had heard stories that U-boats had shelled New York City. He believed there were food shortages in the United States, and that people were able to have only two meals a day. Another of the POWs said that he had read in German papers a year earlier that the Japanese had shelled San Francisco. How surprised they had been to learn that none of the propaganda was true.

Sergeant Testhammer emphasized that all rules of the Geneva convention would be observed. The Germans were to be protected from public curiosity.

The POWs engaged in corn canning at Cokato seven miles away. They were lodged in the fairgrounds which, according to Howard Hong, were not designed for living, but the quarters were equal to regular barracks.

An incident reported in the *Herald* on August 17 put the local populace at ease. "All that shooting that has been heard recently over in the northwest part of town is being done at blackbirds, and not at escaping war prisoners."

One man connected with the use of POW labor in the Cokato area had a special interest in dealing with prisoners of war. German-born Franz Guhl had come to the United States in 1938, and he became an American citizen. When Guhl known as the "seed man" in Dassel was asked to become field boss for the gang of hard-bitten Nazi prisoners, he agreed recalling that five years of his life had been spent in an internment camp. A German citizen residing in India, he had been incarcerated during World War I. His knowledge of the German language and his empathy for the plight of prisoners made him a most sympathetic overseer.

The *Herald* reported on August 24 that the 1944 corn pack was eighty-five percent of normal. Credit was given to the POWs for relieving the labor shortage for the cannery. At that time there were sixty-three captives at the Wright County Fair Grounds. New arrivals had been captured more than a year earlier from the Afrika Korps. They were described as "hard-bitten Nazis."

At the end of the season, the prisoners returned to the base camp at Algona. Again in 1945, Sergeant Testhammer and Military Policemen accompanied 100 POWs to Howard Lake. They again were employed in the corn pack by Northland Cannery Company of Cokato and housed at the Wright County Fairgrounds at Howard Lake.

When the new members of the Wright County Fair took over, they learned that the county commissioners had leased part of the fairgrounds to Northland for the POWs, effective August 1. Dates for the fair were changed to July 27 through 29 so that all buildings and grounds could be used for the exposition before the Germans arrived.

Chapter 19

Camp No. 14, Wells

A public meeting was held in Wells, Minnesota, on June 8, 1945, for a discussion regarding the use of POW labor in the area.

Mayor Manville Oren, Irl Starr of the United States Employment Service and Manpower Commission; Captain Joseph G. Gaitskill, commanding officer of the branch camp at Fairmont; Captain T.K. Herbener, U.S. Army chaplain from the base camp at Algona; Lieutenant Werner P. Schmiedeberg, the new commanding officer at Wells; and Lieutenant Arthur E. Perry, post judge advocate at Algona were present to answer questions proferred by the sixty local people who attended.

It was agreed that there was a manpower shortage in the area. POWs would be able to fill the need. According to Lieutenant Schmiedeberg, "We are here to work and mind our own business, and to get the greatest possible aid from prisoner of war labor, and for no other reason."

Citizens of Wells were reminded of the rules of conduct needed on the part of civilians to guarantee a successful operation. There was to be no fraternization. No photographs could be taken without permission. There was to be no parking of cars nor walking near the camp.

According to the report of an inspection on June 24, 1945, by Major D.L. Schweiger, Provost Marshal General, and Captain C.E. Tremper the camp at Wells, Minnesota, was in operation. It contained nine non-commissioned officers and 245 enlisted men. Quarters for the prisoners were in a former hemp factory building. The captives were put to work in canneries at Wells and at Fairmont. Mike Burns, a Wells plant foreman, said the POWs were good workers, very obedient, and caused no trouble. Most were eighteen- and nineteen-year olds who were taken captive in North Africa. "There were a few SS men. They were more demanding, so we gave them the dirtiest jobs."

Melvin Tatje, a Wells cook room foreman, remembered that there had been some Italian POWs, but said, "They were lazy so they got rid of them." All the supervisors spoke a little German so communication was easy. Prisoners played concertinas during breaks. Cigarettes, which were rationed to civilians, were plentiful for the captives. These were traded for such items as drawing paper. Tatje thought some Germans eventually went to the sugar beet harvest in Colorado.

When work was slack between pea and corn canning, POWs were no longer under contract to the canneries. They then were made available to area farmers. The wage scale was sixty cents per hour plus a charge of forty-five cents per day per man to defray the cost of renting temporary prison camps. Farmers applied for POW labor through the agricultural extension office. They had to provide transportation for the prisoners, and no meals were furnished by the farmer, but an additional twenty-five cents was charged to the farmer for meals taken away from camp. Rations were sent to the Wells camp from Algona. No man could be off the prison grounds for more than fourteen hours at a stretch.

Farmers were asked to determine the day before they wanted help the number of POWs needed for work. Orders were placed with the camp by telephone. Three or more prisoners worked together at a time to harvest crops.

YMCA field secretary Howard Hong visited the Wells installation on August 10, 1945. He noted unusual defeatism by POW leaders in the camp. Many were angry at Adolph Hitler for having committed suicide. Some became depressed on learning the Allied victory and worked less hard.

Hong learned that a YMCA phonograph and records had been received from Algona, which resulted in the start of a small music group. A band was formed with two violins, a saxophone, a guitar, and an accordion. Hong noted that there was no school at the camp. Teachers were available, but there was no space where classes could be conducted. Hong rented brooder houses from a lumber company at a charge of ten dollars for hauling them to the site and five dollars per month for rent. Hong said that if the expense could not be paid by the POW fund, he would go to the prisoner of war aid of the YMCA for the money. Each brooder house held twenty men plus a teacher. Before he departed, the field secretary left fifteen Cassells dictionaries with the commanding officer to help in the establishment of the schools.

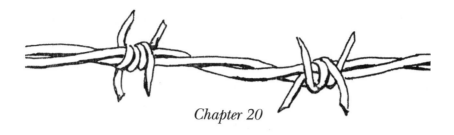

Chapter 20

Camp No. 15, Bird Island

Activated on September 16, 1944, Branch Camp No. 15 at Bird Island was opened for German prisoners of war because of a change in housing regulations set by the United States Army.

The previous year Italian prisoners of war working at Rogers Seed Company of Olivia had been quartered in tents near an old tile factory in that city, and the tents had been deemed unacceptable.

When again in 1944, Rogers Seed Company requested help from prisoners, Germans prisoners of war were transferred from Howard Lake camp. Because of the change in housing regulations, making the tent camp near the old tile factory in Olivia no longer suitable, the POWs were housed in the Renville County fair grounds. They were quartered in buildings on the west front side of the property, and a wire barricade was built down the center of the site to separate the POW camp from the rest of the facility and to prevent escape.

According to Rogers' manager George Sawin, some 100 Germans were expected, along with their guards, probably about ten American soldiers. In September, sixty POWs arrived from Cokato where they had been working on another agricultural project. Five guards under the command of a sergeant accompanied them. A second contingent, which arrived a short time later, brought the total to 100. All had been taken captive early in the fighting in Africa. All were anti-Hitler, feeling that there was no use in Germany continuing to fight. They believed rightly that the Nazi cause was lost.

These prisoners said they liked America very much. They were accorded excellent treatment under the terms of the Geneva Convention, but they were not pampered, though they did get some nice privileges. The *Bird Island Union* of Thursday, September 21, 1944, recorded that on the previous Wednesday the prisoners had enjoyed a movie at the Roxie theater in town.

Speaking in German, the Reverend I.F. Lenz, pastor of Zion Lutheran Church in Olivia, addressed sixty-two POWs in a special Sunday evening service held at the Bird Island headquarters on September 1. After the service, he talked to a number of the prisoners. They said they were well-satisfied with the work of picking seed corn. Several said they knew Germany was defeated and that because of that they were glad to be prisoners of war. All were anxious to learn English and studied the language in their off hours. Many said they wanted to return to the United States after the war was concluded.

The captives worked for the Rogers Seed Company in Olivia for about eight weeks. Each day they were taken by truck from Bird Island to Olivia to work in the seed corn fields. When the field work was finished the POWs returned to the base camp at Algona, Iowa.

By fall of 1945, some American service men had returned home to Olivia but a labor shortage still existed. Again Rogers Brothers obtained German POWs to help them with the harvest. Forty of them arrived August 23 to work at the Olivia Canning Company, and another thirty to work in the fields.

Yvonne Griffin remembered that prisoners worked in her father's fields. Meals in those days consisted of breakfast, dinner, and supper, with a "lunch" delivered by wagon to the fields at mid-morning and mid-afternoon. When the POWs worked at the farm, many of the neighbor women helped prepare the lunches and noon meal. A long trestle table was loaded with fried chicken, mashed potatoes, gravy, ears of sweet corn, fresh tomatoes, pies and cakes.

One of the neighbors, Mrs. Ed Timm, spoke fluent German as did Yvonne's grandmother Mary Hyndman. "Conversations were lively and fast flowing," remembered Yvonne. The POWs were emphatic that they were not German but Austrian. They had been conscripted into the German army with no real belief in the German cause.

"They asked questions about life in America and seemed to be most interested in [the] children, Mary Ann and Herb Timm and myself," Ms. Griffin recalled. "They were so pleased to be treated more like friends by caring people who were just as interested in them and their lives as they were interested in ours. I do not believe that they were made to feel like enemies."

Ms. Griffin remembered a particular incident: "After dinner Mary Ann and Herb got on Grandpa Aurie's big sorrel mare Babe, I on my saddle horse Prince, and we raced after them (the POWs) as they returned to the fields. Prince turned a quick corner. I didn't. When I picked myself up they laughed and laughed, not mean laughter but with joy and delight as if here on the flatlands of Minnesota they were remembering in their hearts their beloved mountains and perhaps a little sister at home."

By the middle of November, work was completed at Rogers Brothers Seed Company. The POWs returned to Algona, Iowa, on November 14, and the Bird Island camp was closed. Manager George Sawin said that the company had used prison labor for the past three seasons, and "this was the best group ever."

Chapter 21

Camp No. 16, Hollandale

Branch Camp No. 16, located near Hollandale in Freeborn County, opened briefly in the autumn of 1944 and again in 1945. The camp was organized October 9, 1944, to help supply farmers with harvest workers. The POWs were under the command of Lt. Robert T. Cumback. While they were in the Hollandale area, the captives topped onions, picked potatoes, and tended to the harvest. The first year, they were quartered in tents about a mile east of the city. The weekly reports for the first year show that 117 POWs were held at Hollandale on October 16 and 23, 116 on November 1.

The Germans all volunteered for the duty. If anyone refused to work Lt. Cumback used what he called "administrative pressure": they were allowed minimal rations and all the water they wanted.

The prisoners did their own laundry, cleaning and cooking. They had their own mess sergeant, who used supplies provided by Fort Snelling. At the end of the 1944 harvest season the captives were returned to the base camp at Algona, Iowa.

In 1945, reports dated November 1 and 16 listed sixty-two prisoners at Camp No. 16. Engaged in agriculture, POWs were harvesting potatoes, sugar beets, and carrots. They were also used in the collection and production of hemp, which was grown in the area.

Four of the 100 POWs in the Hollandale area in 1945 are shown at the John Reynen farm. The Germans volunteered for the duty. (Photo courtesy of Al and Doris Reynen)

That year, the Germans were quartered outside of town at a site on the south side of the road about a mile south and a half-mile east of Hollandale. The buildings, six or eight of them, were constructed of wood and canvas. Floors of wood were enclosed with six-foot high walls topped with two-by-four framing. Canvas tenting covered the framing, forming roofs for the barracks. After the war, the buildings were completed, and the bunkhouses were used for several years as lodging for migrant Mexican workers. Eventually the whole camp was torn down.

Farmers who used POW labor were required to furnish the prisoners with their noon meal and to return them to the prison camp at the end of each day. POWs assigned to farm work found themselves offered home-cooked meals from the families who employed them. The farmers felt that men worked almost as hard as their regular hired help so should be fed as well also.

One group of captives was assigned to the Engel and Jean Nienoord farm near Hollandale. According to Jean Nienoord, some POWs seemed happy to have been captured. Some of the internees, on the other hand, were true Nazis and never cracked a smile. They were hard men. "Others were very nice," she said.

One of these was Ernest Kohleich, who was captured in March 1945, two months before Germany surrendered. He returned to Hollandale in 1976. At that time, Lois West, staff writer for the *Albert Lea Tribune* interviewed him. Kohleich said that after his capture, he and his fellow prisoners had been taken first to France, then to Southampton, England, where they boarded a convoy of 120 American ships. They arrived in New York on May 16, eight days after V-E Day. Put on a train, they were sent to the main POW camp at Algona, Iowa. Kohleich was in the group assigned to the branch camp at Whitewater State Park. He said he worked in a cannery. Later, he was among those taken to the Hollandale area to help with the vegetable harvest in September and October of 1945.

Kohleich said that living conditions were good, "as far as one has living conditions as a POW." He said that he was glad he was alive and not injured. "I was also glad I had learned English and could read and understand. On the other hand, I didn't know if my parents were alive. I knew our home was destroyed in an air raid in 1943." Food in the POW camp was good and was prepared according to German standards, said Kohleich. People were kind to them, "treating us as though we were of the same class."

Jean Nienoord recalled, "We'd sit on the back of the truck and converse." She added that she and her husband would share cookies and other baked goods with the POWs. Since Kohleich was the only one who could speak English, a special friendship developed. That friendship resulted in the 1976 pilgrimage on which Koehlich brought his wife, Ursel, son Reinhard, and daughter Dorothee.

Since his 1976 visit, Kohleich remembered that in 1945 the United States Army captain at Whitewater had had to sign papers confirming that the German POWs had seen newspapers printed in their native language. The reports revealed some of the horrors of Nazi Germany, such as the concentration camps at Auschwitz and Dachau. "I was ashamed these things happened and disappointed that I had been indoctrinated by this ideology."

Nienrood said that while the POWs were working on the farm in 1945, she invited them to eat with her. "I kind of felt sorry for them." When one asked her why Americans treated the pris-

German prisoners of war harvesting carrots on the John Reynen farm near Hollandale. Reynen said his family worked right alongside the prisoners. (Photo courtesy of Al and Doris Reynen)

oners so well, she told him of her brother who was fighting in Europe. "He was in the service, and I said that if he was captured I hoped he would be treated likewise. I told them that I was taught by my father that we should love our enemy."

Japanese prisoners of war also were quartered in the Hollandale neighborhood on August 28, 1945. En route to Camp McCoy, Wisconsin, from Clarinda, Iowa, where they had been working, the POWs stopped at Horace Austin State Park in Austin. Accompanied by three guards, they swatted mosquitoes while they ate sandwiches and chattered in their native language. One of the guards who had worked with both German and Japanese POWs talked to a reporter from the *Austin Daily Herald*. He said that the Japanese were easier to handle. They obeyed orders implicitly, whereas the Germans tended to argue.

He said that the Japanese took it very hard when their nation surrendered. However, the surrender improved the status of the prisoners. The Japanese soldier believed that permitting himself to be captured caused him to be banished from his homeland forever. After Japan surrendered, the chances for the POWs' return with honor to their homeland improved.

In the fall of 1945, several German POWs located at the Hollandale camp were assigned to help the Olin Hamer family in the harvesting of sugar beets, potatoes, and onions. The Hamer farm was located near the outlet of Geneva Lake between Clarks Grove and Hollandale. Shirley Hamer, then just a youngster, recalled going with her father to the Hollandale camp to pick up several prisoners.

Hamer and other farmers checked out the number of captives they needed to help with their harvest season. According to Shirley and her mother, there were no guards to watch the prisoners as they worked in the fields. "In a way, the entire operation was run on an honor system," Shirley said.

One of the POWs, Wilhelm Paecher, was particularly friendly. "He's the only one we really recall," said Shirley. She had posed for a photo with Wilhelm Paecher in the Hamer sugar beet field.

Shirley Hamer poses with Wilhelm Paecher, a POW from the camp near Hollandale. In October 1945, several prisoners were assigned to work in the sugar beet field owned by Olin Hamer, Shirley's father. (Courtesy of the *Albert Lea Tribune*)

Al Reynen had POWs help in September and October of 1945. His four helpers were part of a group of about 100 housed in a barracks about one-half mile east of Hollandale in a building that is now a potato warehouse.

The POWs harvested potatoes, onions, and carrots at the Reynen farm. According to Reynen, one twenty-year-old had lost his toes in the campaign against Russia. One had been a sergeant, and he did not take orders too well. The other two were family men and were more easy-going.

Said Raynen, "We gave them a good meal of potatoes and vegetables at noon." After news of German atrocities to American prisoners became known, the rations at the prisoner-of-war camp were cut.

Regarding the relationship between prisoners and the farmers, Reynen said, "We worked right along with them. We got along fine with them. They were fairly good workers considering the situation."

The POWs were transferred to other camps after the crops in the Hollandale area were put up.

Chapter 22

The 1945 Harvest Camps

A LATE GROWING SEASON AND BUMPER CROPS of sugar beets and potatoes strained the labor shortage experienced in Minnesota agriculture in 1945. Though migrant Mexican workers had come through the area earlier, the bulk of the crops matured after the Mexican workers returned home.

Farmers in the Crookston area contracted for POW labor and looked forward to the arrival of forty prisoners the first week in October to aid in the potato harvest. They were quartered in the winter sports arena. The internees came from the branch camp at Montgomery where they had worked in a cannery. Captain Clyde W. Snider, who became commanding officer of the camp, and Sgt. Seal inspected the quarters. A local doctor was contracted to provide medical treatment for the captives while they were in Crookston.

The *Crookston Daily Times* reported on October 5, 1945, that carpenters, plumbers—even local business men—were working to get the arena ready for the POWs. A lavatory was installed, and the Army provided stoves for cooking and heat. Guards brought most of the necessary equipment for housing of the POWs—bedding and mess equipment as well as trucks for transporting the Germans to and from the fields. The men slept in double-decker bunks.

The prisoners were under constant guard, and the public was warned that no loitering would be permitted near the arena. Dean Wiley, secretary of the Crookston Chamber of Commerce, asked that the public stay away from the sports arena for thirty days while the POWs were in town. On arrival, which was antici-pated with some eagerness because the POWs were seen as the farmers' "last resort" to alleviate the labor problem, the prisoners were divided among the various potato producers for field work.

Food was provided by the Army. Cooks were available from among the prisoner population, and POWs were served family style meals, usually consisting of mashed potatoes, steamed cabbage, bread, stewed fruit, and coffee.

Censorship was tight. Mail sent in and out of the camp was opened, and even magazines were screened.

Chapel services were conducted in the arena on Wednesdays by the Reverend Millard T. Wolfram of Emanuel Lutheran Church of East Grand Forks. Catholic Mass was held on Sundays.

On October 11th, 125 more POWs arrived to help in har-vesting potatoes.

The POWs remained in the Crookston area until the first part of November. During this critical harvest, they earned $138,517.18 for the United States government in payment from farmers for their work.

After a mass influx of paid civilian workers to the potato fields because of higher wages, sugar beet producers in Ada, Minnesota, appealed to Minnesota Governor Edward Thye for even more help. More than 1,000 acres of beets had yet to be har-vested. The governor contacted Seventh Service Command Headquarters at Omaha, Nebraska. Charles Callahan arrived in Ada from the headquarters early in October accompanied by Captain Clyde W. Snider, commanding officer of the Crookston camp. They met with the sugar beet growers, Junior Chamber of Commerce, city officials, and Senator Norman Larson at the Norman County courthouse. It was agreed that a prisoner of war camp would be set up at the fairgrounds in Ada. The cost of set-ting up this camp was borne by the sugar beet growers, who paid sixty cents an hour to the government for the work done by each prisoner, with each POW receiving eighty cents a day.

Approximately 200 POWs arrived on Saturday, October 13, at 8:30 A.M. on a special train accompanied by U.S. Army guards.

Internees were housed in the coliseum at the fair grounds, eating at a nearby dining hall. They started work in the fields on Monday morning and remained until the early part of November to complete the harvest. Growers estimated that 1,000 acres of potatoes awaited harvest. Originally the potatoes were planted for use in the war effort so the Army felt obligated to insure safe processing of the crop, according to Lieutenant Colonel Lobdell.

The Warren, Minnesota, *Sheaf* reported on October 3, 1945, that Mexican laborers would not return for the sugar beet and potato harvest. The late season was given as the reason. This resulted in a critical shortage of labor. It was reported that 400 POWs were expected to arrive from the base camp at Algona and from the branch camp at Wells, which had been closed. POWs would be housed in buildings of the North Star Bible College Association, reported the *Sheaf.* The Army would provide food, cots, and bedding, and the camp would be enclosed with a barbed wire fence.

The newspaper reported a week later that prisoners had arrived by Great Northern railroad. The contingent was not 400 Germans, but rather 200 Italians. The additional 200 POWs were not sent to Warren, however, because housing was not sufficient to accommodate them. Working in crews of twenty men, they harvested for two days on one farm, then were transferred to another. Good weather aided the harvest.

While at work in the sugar beet harvest, Italians POWs on the Heismer Pearson field northwest of Alvarado saved the life of Edwin Anderson, a tractor operator. He was drawing a float over the beet field when his machine tipped upside down in a ditch pinning him underneath. The POWs raced to the scene, raised the tractor and dragged Anderson out from under it. Gas leaking from the fuel tank ignited, but the POWs shoveled dirt onto the tractor to put out the fire. They saved the machine—and Anderson's life.

With the beet harvest finished early in November, the POW camp at Warren was discontinued. The POWs, with twenty guards and staff, left by train for Osage, Iowa, their permanent camp. Of their help in the harvest, potato contractors and sugar beet producers termed the work of the Italians variously as "satisfactory" and "excellent."

On October 18, Lieutenant Colonel Arthur Lobdell, commanding officer of the base camp at Algona, Iowa, said that prisoners of war would save the sugar beet crop and the potato crop. Branch camps of German POWs were opened at Grafton and Grand Forks, North Dakota, as well as at Crookston, and Ada, Minnesota.

Between October 7 and November 6, 1945, 1,458 German and Italian POWs worked to save the $4,140,000 crop of sugar beets and potatoes. The POWs harvested thirty-four percent of that crop, valued at some $1,407,600. Said Lieutenant Colonel Lobdell, "A near miracle was accomplished in the Red River Valley through the use of POWs." He added, "The production job in the Red River Valley was one of the best that the POWs out of this base camp have done. He cautioned that the prisoners would not be around the following year. Potato and sugar beet crops would have to be harvested by American labor.

In a letter to Lobdell, P.E. Miller, director of agriculture extension work in Minnesota, said that rather than thinking in terms of saving the whole crop, farmers were concerned with what percentage could be saved. Miller extended heartiest thanks

By June 1945, the United States had realized more than $102 million from the work done by POWs in this country. Here, German prisoners of war work in the fields of the Henry Peterson Farm near Moorhead, Minnesota. (Courtesy of the Henry Peterson Farm Papers, Northwest Minnesota Historical Center, Moorhead, Minnesota)

on behalf of the farmers. Carl G. Ash, county agricultural agent for Polk County, Minnesota, said that most of the potatoes and sugar beets would not have been harvested without POW help. Outstanding cooperation was exhibited between the American employers and branch camp officers in directing the prisoners. There were no reports of ill feeling.

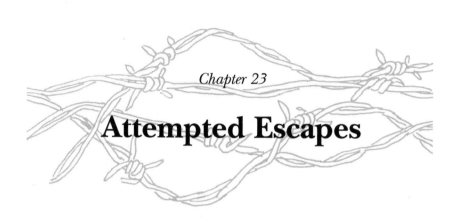

Chapter 23

Attempted Escapes

UNDER THE TERMS OF THE GENEVA CONVENTION of 1929, it was the duty of a prisoner of war to try to escape. For a POW in the United States, the situation was next to impossible. If he were to elude capture, where would he go? It was more than a thousand miles to the nearest ocean, and the Atlantic Ocean separated him from his homeland.

No underground networks existed in the United States as they did in Europe to channel the escapee to friends and freedom. POW camps were quite secure, with barbed-wire-topped fences containing the captives. Guards patrolled the premises day and night, and spotlights left few dark corners in the camps in which to hide or dig tunnels.

Prisoners of war gave their American captors little trouble in the internment camps. They were escorted to and from their places of employment, and they wore marked clothing, with a "PW" stenciled on the back, which would be easy to spot in a civilian population. Some said the white letters would make a good target if a POW did escape.

Most prisoners were content to be out of the war, well-fed, adequately clothed and housed and working in peaceful surroundings. POW camps sometimes were referred to as "The Fritz Ritz." The internee had better food as a POW than he had had in the German Army. He had access to a PX and canteen where sometimes wine and beer were available. Newspapers, concerts, and plays were presented by the prisoners. Many took correspondence courses through local universities. Even though the men were confined it was a tolerable life.

Though the prisoners had been taken out of the war, they were still soldiers and there was still a tight military unity. Each rank was responsible to its superiors. The American Army felt it most efficient to let the POW officers control their own men. But escapes were beyond the scope of this military organization.

The first prisoners were sent to Northern Minnesota in December of 1943. Authorities decided that the barbed wire fencing could wait until the pulpwood was cut. To discourage escape attempts, the guards told tall tales of the wolves, bears, stags, and porcupines inhabiting the wilderness. They told of wild Indians in the neighborhood. One POW wrote home saying that "deserting was quite impossible as too many wolves and Indians, ill-disposed to white people, are running around here." He continued, "The Indians drink, swing the tomahawk, and go to war."

Still there were a few who attempted to leave their prisons. Some of the would-be escapees simply had cabin fever. They wanted more room to move around, wanted to see the cities and escape boredom. Some wanted to meet girls. Professional soldiers, of course, felt it was their patriotic duty to escape. At the end of the war, prisoners who learned they would be going home to East Germany knew they would return to Russian occupation—the worst fate imaginable, in their minds, and were tempted to try to escape and disappear into the civilian world.

Statistics given in the Glenville, Minnesota, *Progress* on May 18, 1944, revealed a total of 183,618 prisoners in camps in the United States. Of this number 133,135 were Germans, 50,136 were Italians, and 347 were Japanese. To that date, only 285 had attempted to escape. As of May 3, only five were still at large.

On Friday, May 26, 1944, the Mankato (Minnesota) *Free Press* carried an article stating that police were on the lookout for two German prisoners who were reported to have escaped from the base camp at Algona, Iowa. The FBI warned that they were probably headed for southern Minnesota. Both were wearing

German uniforms without POWs identification. Harri Schipp-mann, age twenty-one, was five foot, nine inches tall, weighed 175 pounds, had brown eyes and hair, a fair complexion, and a scar on his right hand. He was wearing a khaki shirt with lapels, olive drab breeches, leggings, and government-issue shoes. Schipp-mann spoke English. His companion, Karl Braun, was twenty-four, six feet tall, and 147 pounds, with blue eyes, fair complexion, and wearing blue trousers, a khaki shirt, leggings, and GI shoes.

Historian George Lobdell, nephew of the second commander of Camp Algona, Lieutenant Colonel Arthur T. Lobdell, recounted the event.

Guards were posted around the double-fenced stockade. Because of the shortage of guards, the middle tower was not manned. The two POWs dug a hole under the inner fence near the vacant tower, and then cut some strands of wire in the outer fence. After crawling under it, they repaired the wire so well that it wasn't noticed for several days.

Apparently, local residents called the camp twice to report the escape, but camp officials double-checked the roster and found no one missing.

The following day, the FBI reported that the two Germans had been recaptured by the city marshall in West Bend, sixteen miles away. Later it was learned that the numbers of prisoners on work details were supplied by German clerks. They had produced fictitious figures to cover for the missing pair.

Still later, there was a report that the pair had never made it out of the camp. They supposedly had hidden in a stockade latrine for a day.

A second escape was made by Alois Stephan. After slipping out of camp through a culvert, he walked two miles to Algona. There he surprised Clarence Frazier as he was sweeping the sidewalk in front of his pool hall. Stephan turned himself in, then waited inside the recreation hall for the sheriff to arrive.

The Algona newspaper reported, "It seems the policy of the Nazi prisoners is to get guards to lose face with the home people. The fact that the prisoners go out of their way to be picked up gives credence to that idea."

Within days of that fiasco, Colonel Joseph Church, the camp commander, had been reassigned. He was replaced by Lieutenant Colonel Lobdell, who remained in charge until the camp closed in February 1946.

The northern part of Minnesota was put on alert by the FBI early in July 1944. At that time, a bulletin was issued for two Nazi prisoners who escaped from a work camp fifty miles east of Fort Francis, Ontario, across the bridge from International Falls. Tout Wallner, age twenty-one, was five feet, four inches tall, weighed 120 pounds, had brown eyes, and light brown hair. With him was Alexander Treu, twenty-four, six feet, one inch tall, with blue eyes, and brown hair. Treu spoke both German and English. The Royal Canadian Mounted Police believed the two had managed to cross into the United States. On July 11, 1944, according to the *Faribault Daily News,* the FBI announced that the two prisoners from the Canadian camp had been captured by the mounties while trying to get into the United States.

A terse comment records another escape attempt, this one at the camp near Fairmont, Minnesota. On July 9 and 10 Albrecht Gick and Leo Scheltner were sentenced to twenty days confinement and seven days on bread and water "for leaving camp and for irregularities in their correspondence."

Warroad, Minnesota, was on the alert for an escapee on August 25, 1944. Joseph Petzelt, a German POW from a camp near Kenora, Ontario, Canada, was being hunted by customs, immigration, and forestry personnel. Petzelt had been seen the previous day by Neil Leitch of Hawes Island, who had given the man some food. On learning of the POW's identity, Leicht contacted authorities, advising them that Petzelt had a map of Lake of the Woods. Petzelt was five foot, six inches tall, with blue eyes and dark brown hair. At the time of his escape, he was wearing overalls, a gray shirt, and a straw hat.

Four days later, the Austin (Minnesota) *Daily Herald* carried the report that Petzelt was in the custody of immigration authorities. On Monday morning, a Booth fisheries boat under the command of Lawerence Saurdiff had come upon a man in a twelve-foot canoe made from a hollowed-out poplar log. The man was not armed and offered no resistance as he and his canoe were loaded aboard the fishing boat.

Petzelt was reported to have a good supply of food, clothing, and blankets, and he had caught a fine supply of fish. He admitted that his plan was to cross Lake of the Woods into the United States and get work on a farm. His escape ended four days after it started.

An escape from the Interlaken camp near Fairmont took place on Sunday, September 24, 1944. Three German captives simply walked away. Their explanation for their departure from camp: "We heard music across the lake at Amber Inn. It was a nice night. We thought we'd go over." The trio walked around Amber Lake, then "borrowed" a row boat using boards as paddles to return across the lake to the camp.

Two of the walk-aways returned voluntarily. The third was captured by Paul Sigmund who recognized him as a prisoner. The escapee was taken to the Martin County jail and returned to the base camp at Algona, Iowa. He was to be sent to a camp for incorrigible prisoners.

Joseph E. Gaitskill of the Corps of Military Police, commanding officer of the camp at Fairmont, later spoke to the College Women's Club of that city. He said, "The recalcitrant young German who decided to spend a night out of the stockade in Fairmont was sent to Algona and given fourteen days on bread and water. Punishment must be administrative, not punitive." This was in accord with the Geneva convention. Escape by a prisoner was regarded as a breach of discipline, not a crime. It was punishable by up to thirty days confinement, fourteen of them on bread and water.

The escapee returned by Sigmund originally had been taken prisoner at Cherbourg. He had been drafted into the Nazi army at age seventeen. Two weeks after his capture, he was in the United States. An only child, his parents had been killed and his home destroyed by bombing. His uncle was killed on the Russian front. This was the "recalcitrant young German."

Two workers in the Faribault camp walked away after drinking seven or eight bottles of 3.2 beer in the canteen. Robert Strache and Alfred Oligmuller were returning to camp quite happy with their brief escapade when they were arrested by local police.

Perhaps the best documented escape was that of Oberge-freiter (corporal) Walter Mai and Obergrenadier (private first class) Heinz Schymalla, who left the camp near Bena on Saturday night, October 28, 1944. They had been in Minnesota about nine months and knew that the tales of wild Indians, wolves, and bears were mere fabrications designed to keep the prisoners in camp. Mai, twenty-one, five foot, eleven inches tall, had fair skin and dark blond hair. He had been a farmer before entering the German Army. A member of the Afrika Korps, he was captured by the British in Tunisia in 1943. Schymalla, twenty-two, was five foot seven inches tall, with fair skin and brown hair. He had been a laborer before entering the army, and was captured by the Americans in Tunisia. Neither spoke more than a few phrases of English.

The POWs learned that Allied victories had liberated France, Belgium, Luxembourg, and part of the Netherlands, and that American forces were about to attack Hitler's Siegfried line. Schymalla received a letter from home telling him that his sixty-year-old father and a brother had been drafted into military service. This news made Schymalla decide it was time for him to try to return home and help his country.

Discovering that Walter Mai was of the same mind, Schmyalla began to plot their escape, using a small map of the United States found in a dictionary to make plans. The pair managed to acquire some unmarked clothing kept in the camp supply room. Each day they saved food from their rations. At length they had accumulated bacon, sausage, sugar, butter, and other items. With the help of their companions, they managed to save four loaves of bread. They also made a slingshot with which they hoped to kill small game for food.

Bena prisoners had been allowed to build about a dozen small boats from scrap lumber. Schymalla and Mai reasoned that since the Mississippi River flowed to New Orleans, they could find a neutral ship in the Gulf of Mexico and sail for home. They hid one of the flimsy, home-made boats, the *Lili Marlene #10*, in the weeds on the lakeshore. Then the two prisoners packed bags and a suitcase with blankets, pillows, extra clothes, shoes, and boots. They took along such items as a chess set, cigarettes, matches, books, pills, and shaving equipment.

The gate of the compound was left unlocked until 10:00 P.M. each night to allow those captives who worked outside the camp to return from their jobs. On Saturday, the final prisoner count was made at 11:00 P.M., and there was no bed check on Sundays.

On Saturday night, Schymalla and Mai went to bed wearing their unmarked clothing. At 10:45 P.M., Captain Clifford Jenner, commanding officer of the camp, and his American guards toured the barracks, then locked the stockade gate for the night. It wasn't long before Schmyalla and Mai stole away. At the edge of camp they waited for the lone guard to pass, then shoved their luggage under the fence and crawled to freedom. At Lake Winnibogoshish, they loaded their gear into their boat and traveled about five miles before daylight forced them to land. There they hid through Sunday.

The disappearance of Schymalla and Mai was not discovered until late Sunday evening. Camp officials did not have a correct count of the boats, so they failed to notice that one was missing. The ranking German sergeant made a preliminary bed check and found a note: "Our Fatherland, Our Homeland are now in a very difficult position, and need all available sons, and therefore we will try to arrive at our homeland." The note ended with a promise not to commit any sabotage, and wished "for the whole camp in Bena for the future the best."

On learning of the escape, Captain Clifford Jenner ordered a search of the entire camp. When the missing men were not located, Jenner ordered the escape alert plan put into action. Sirens were sounded. Guards searched the surrounding area. The FBI in Minneapolis was notified. Sheriffs in nearby counties were put on alert. Lieutenant Colonel Arthur Lobdell at Algona, Iowa, was informed of the breakout.

And what of the escapees? Temperatures were in the low thirty-degree range, and a storm delayed their journey. Still they made it through Little Winnibigoshish Lake, down the Mississippi through White Oak Lake. When they reached Jay Gould Lake, they made a mistake. Instead of following the current of the river, they paddled into the lake.

Resort owner J.G. Shoup saw them and wondered who they were. Shoup rowed out after the two. When he questioned the men, Schymilla answered in limited English. Suspicious, Shoup returned to shore and telephoned the sheriff's office in Grand Rapids.

The fugitives suspected they had been detected and decided to abandon the boat. They packed their supplies into bundles and started hiking. They hadn't gone far when Deputy Sheriff Otto Litchke, Grand Rapids Chief of Police George Crock and former state highway patrolman John Murray drove onto the road near them.

The Germans hid in the bushes. Litchke and Crock searched the area while Murray guarded the car. Figuring they were surrounded, Mai and Schymalla decided to surrender. The men were driven to the county jail in Grand Rapids, and the FBI and Army authorities were notified. The escapees were promptly taken to Algona.

After a hearing, Lieutant Colonel Lobdell sentenced them each to thirty days confinement, with fourteen days on a diet of bread and water. The fugitives had been free for five and a half days. They had traveled more than fifty miles down the Mississippi River, but were just thirty-five miles away from the Bena Camp when recaptured.

An investigation by the military committee of House of Representatives of Congress said that escape attempts by prisoners of war were surprisingly small. At that time, there were 281,344 Germans, 51,032 Italians, and 2,242 Japanese in the United States.

A short-lived escape was that of August Heulle who walked way from the camp at Owatonna on January 13, 1945. The bed check disclosed that he was missing, and a search was underway. He returned about 11:00 P.M. on his own.

According to Major General Archer L. Lerch, Provost Marshal General, by March 12, 1945, fifty-six POWs had been shot trying to escape. Of a total of 1,350 escape attempts throughout the United States, all but six Germans and six Italians were back in custody by March 1. Most of the escapes were walk-aways from jobs.

Two residents of the Bena camp escaped under the fence after dark on April 27, 1945. Kurt Touey and Joachim Starkoff apparently wished to avoid being separated from each other in a transfer scheduled for the next day. To avoid this, they left the camp. Their absence was discovered at bed check, and they were taken into custody about six miles from the camp.

A search was underway throughout southern Minnesota and Wisconsin early in July 1945. Two Japanese prisoners had escaped from Camp McCoy, Wisconsin. On Tuesday, July 5, Hirasawa Mitsuhei, age thirty-five, five foot, five inches tall, and weighing 137 pounds, escaped. The following night, Masao Kitaura, age twenty-four, five foot, four inches tall and 135 pounds made it out of the camp. Both were wearing POW uniforms, which gave them a difficult time trying to blend into the populace.

According to Dr. George H. Lodbell, nephew of Lieutenant Colonel Arthur Lobdell, several POWs slipped away from camp for short periods of time undetected.

Werner Meinel, who returned to the United States after the war and became a citizen, revealed that he left Camp Algona one evening in 1944 and met a secretary from the camp hospital. After she and her brother drove him around the city, they returned him to the stockade where he sneaked back in.

Prisoner Volker Schweda said he had left the Owatonna camp twice and returned undetected. A prisoner at the St. Charles, Minnesota, branch camp had three Sunday trysts with an American woman. His escapades would have gone unnoticed had he not come down with a venereal disease.

Several days after the end of the war, Werner Meinel, Peter Fritz, and Volker Schweda walked away from the camp at Owatonna, apparently to get a taste of Americana before they were repatriated. They visited the county fair, and Meinel rode the ferris wheel, bought a sandwich, and played a game before he was picked up by civilian police. The other two were apprehended when they returned to camp early in the morning.

Generally, escapes were not much of a problem. As reported by Albert Wild, Plainview, Minnesota, former general manager of the Lakeside Canning Company, "I had two very hard core Nazis that were SS troops. They were always planning an escape and trying to get the other prisoners to go along. They were finally both taken care of." This probably meant that they were sent back to the base camp at Algona.

Wild also recalled that while on a routine check of the cannery, he found one of the camp guards asleep with his rifle across his knees. One of the German POWs told Wild he could have made an escape attempt by stealing the guard's rifle. He overlooked the chance because he was very grateful to be a prisoner in America. Most of the POWs were content to be out of the war and stayed behind the barbed wire fences.

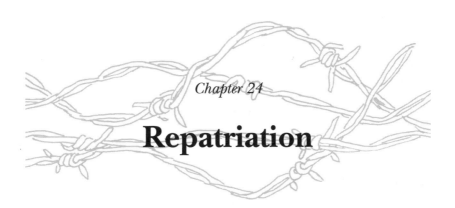

Chapter 24

Repatriation

GERMANY SURRENDERED UNCONDITIONALLY to the Allies on May 7, 1945. The surrender was signed in General Dwight D. Eisenhower's headquarters in Rheims, France, by Col. Gen. Gustav Jodl for Germany, and for the Allies by Lt. Gen. W.B. Smith, Eisenhower's Chief of Staff. Gen. Ivan Susloparoff signed for the Soviet Union, and Gen. Francois Sevez for France.

On August 14, 1945, the unconditional surrender of Japan was announced by President Harry S. Truman. The surrender document was signed aboard the *U.S.S. Missouri* in Tokyo Bay by Foreign Minister Mamoru Shigemitsu and General Yoshijiro Umezu for Japan; General Douglas MacArthur and Admiral Chester Nimitz for the United States. Representatives of other nations followed. The date of the actual signing was September 2, Tokyo time, September 1, Eastern War Time.

On September 15, 1945, there were 362,170 German prisoners of war in the United States, as well as 49,784 Italian, and 5,080 Japanese prisoners. No guidelines had been set at the Geneva Convention for repatriation in the event of unconditional surrender. It only provided for return of prisoners as part of an armistice. As the tide of war turned after the invasion of Normandy in June 1944, the number of captured soldiers was so huge it was impossible to keep track of them. On October 27, Chief of Staff George C. Marshall ordered General Dwight D.

Eisenhower to stop shipping prisoners to the United States. He halted the flow to try to plan for repatriation.

As early as September 7, 1944, J. Cameron Thompson, chairman of the Minnesota War Service Fund, said that full exchange of prisoners of war would not be completed for at least a full year after the war in Europe ended—perhaps even longer. According to information from John R. Mott, chairman of the War Prisoners Aid Committee, the exchange was to be reciprocal and would be based on such considerations as transportation, diplomatic negotiations, social and economic conditions in the countries to which the POWs were returning, and the physical condition of the captives. Thompson said that morale problems would be inevitable after the war ceased. POWs couldn't see why they could not be returned immediately.

In 1945 after a great deal of discussion, the War Department set guidelines for the return of prisoners to their homelands. German prisoners in the United States at the time of the German collapse were to be returned to Europe as soon as possible to be retained in custody there, paroled, or repatriated and released. Those retained in custody would be under control of any of the several allied nations involved. Employable United States-"owned" prisoners would be used on the continent to meet labor requirements of the occupation. Surplus prisoners would be made available for transfer to other European United Nations countries. Non-commissioned officers and incorrigible Nazis were to be the last to be released from prisoner-of-war status.

There were arguments for and against the policies. Some said that prisoners kept in the United States were taking jobs that should go to returning American soldiers. Others argued that there still was a need for POWs to help the United States labor scene. In Minnesota, farmers were not happy to see the captives returned to their homeland because they needed prisoner labor to harvest crops. The same was true for the pulpwood industry in the northern part of the state.

Sentiments were expressed that prisoners should be used to rebuild the lands they had devastated. There was concern by the military government in Germany that the return of the prisoners would have a negative effect on that country because food supplies were low. It was also feared that the ex-prisoners would join the malcontents against the Allied rule in Germany. The civilian population in Germany resented the returnees. Most of the prisoners who had been in the United States had been better fed than the German civilians; most of them had gained weight while in captivity. They were healthier than those who had endured the war under the Third Reich.

Restrictions were set as to what the returning prisoners could take home. An allowance of thirty pounds of luggage was set for enlisted men, 175 pounds for officers. No American currency could be taken from the country. Profits from the POW canteens were to be distributed. Trust and savings accounts set up for the captives who worked in this country were liquidated. The prisoners were given government checks, usually about fifty dollars. Some officers had accumulated several hundred dollars.

The port of embarkation was Camp Shanks, New York. From there it was a nine-day trip to Le Havre. About 3,000 POWs were placed on each ship. Usually the returnees were given to the Allies for their work force. The Allies used them in coal mines, as longshoremen, and as day laborers.

Wilhelm Paecher of Hofgeismer, Germany, who had been interned near Owatonna and temporarily at Hollandale, wrote to farmer Olin Hamer of that community several years after the war. He said that he had left the United States in November 1945, expecting to be returned home. "It was a great surprise tome when I arrived in France instead of going home. I was sent to the coal mines." It was only after three years hard work that he finally arrived home. Even after that length of time, people were still suffering from the war. Poverty and hunger still stalked the land. Prices were very high and wages very low. Paecher found work as a cement layer.

Official photo of Wilhelm Paecher of Hofgeismer, Germany, taken while he was assigned to a camp south of Hollandale, Minnesota. (Photo courtesy of Shirley Hamer and the *Albert Lea Tribune*)

Wilhelm Paecher, center, in 1996 sent greetings from Hofgeismer, Germany, to Shirley Hamer of Hollandale, Minnesota. Paecher was a POW assigned to work on the Hamer farm in the fall of 1945. Paecher's wife stands second from the left. The other women are his wife's sisters. Contact between Paecher and the Hamers was made through the help of a German war bride. (Photo courtesy of Shirley Hamer and the *Albert Lea Tribune*)

Some former POWs replaced American troops in maintenance work. The British kept POWs to do mine-sweeping in the waters around their island after the war was over. Technically, they didn't have the right to do this, but many former prisoners stayed voluntarily.

After the war, a New Ulm farmer continued to write to one of the prisoners who had worked for him. The former captive confirmed that it took some POWs up to three years to get back to Germany. Many were held in camps in France, Scotland, and Great Britain and used as a cheap labor force.

Once in Europe, the prisoners were fingerprinted and processed by the United States Army for the last time. Personnel files were completed. All of these records for prisoners who had been incarcerated in the United States eventually were returned to the Federal Republic of Germany.

The first prisoners were sent home about August 10, 1945. By November 20, 1945, only 73,178 Germans had been repatriated. A schedule was set up to get the rest home as soon as possible. By the end of March 1946, just 140,606 captives were left in the United States. That number was reduced to 37,491 by the end of May.

The plan was to have all of them returned to Europe by Spring of 1946. Actually it wasn't until July 23 of that year that the last German prisoner departed from the United States.

When they reached home, the former POWs found ruin, destruction, and desolation. Lieutenant S.N. Swisher, Jr., of Bayport, Minnesota, was a United States Army medical officer on transit duty between New York and Europe. He wrote in February 1946, that on a recent trip 1,400 Italian POWs were taken to Naples, Italy. While they were enthusiastic about getting home, they were very disappointed to see poverty and wreckage in their homeland. It was a totally different world than they had known as prisoners of war in the United States. Whereas POWs had been living quite well in camps in the United States, there was a great lack of food in Europe. Swisher wrote that relief food went to the black market, often stolen by the national police charged with the responsibility for its distribution. The same was true, he said, for German POWs returned through France.

Many of the former POWs had been so impressed with the United States that they returned when they were able. Some came to visit, some to live.

In America's Bicentennial year, Whitewater State Park received a visit from Ernst Kohleich. Twenty-one years earlier, he had been a nineteen-year-old prisoner of war assigned to work in the harvest fields near Hollendale. In 1976, he was a teacher in Germany of English literature, Latin, and religion. On his nos-

Camera in hand, Ernst Kohleich, right, toured the Hollandale, Minnesota, area where he had worked in 1945 as a prisoner of war. Mrs. Jean Nienoord had befriended the young soldier, and the Koelichs visited Mrs. Nienoord, left, in 1976. With Koelich are his son, Reinhard, daughter, Dorothee, and wife, Ursel. (Photo courtesy of the *Albert Lea Tribune*)

talgic trip, he brought with him his wife, Ursel, and his family. All that remained of POW Camp No. 10 was a single water storage tank on a hill. Not a sign of the old barracks remained. Even the old railroad tracks where the prisoners had loaded onions and cabbages onto boxcars were no longer used. Kohleick had been captured by the Americans in March 1945 and sent to the Minnesota POW camp. He wanted to show his family the place of his internment. He stated that the state park was "about the best place to be held prisoner." The family agreed that Whitewater was very beautiful.

Another former POW, Hans Wilker had been assigned to the lumbering area near Deer River. He liked the community so well that he returned in 1953. He lived there for fifteen years before going to California.

A former internee at Cottonwood camp near New Ulm also became an American citizen. A native of Schweidnitz, Herbert Richter had been a radio operator in the German Air Force. At age nineteen he was captured and sent to Minnesota. He said no one wanted to escape because they felt safe out of the war. Richter wanted to stay in the United States after the war but said only doctors and engineers were permitted to do so. He was able to return later and settled in Kenosha, Wisconsin.

Another who came back was Alfred Mueller. He was drafted into the Luftwaffe in 1938 at age eighteen. A radio lineman, he worked in Holland, Belgium, France, Czechoslovakia, and Russia. He was captured in Tunisia and spent most of his internment at Algona, Iowa. He returned to Berlin in June 1946, and found both parents were dead. The city was devastated. His family was in East Berlin. Mueller emigrated to the United States, returning to Algona, the city of his captivity. He lived for a time in Minneapolis, then retired to Faribault, Minnesota. Mueller attended the reunion of the American 34th Division, the unit against which he fought in Tunisia.

One POW who has not returned yet was Wilhelm Paecher. He may still do so. On February 10, 1996, contact was established between the former POW and the American farm family for whom he had worked while a prisoner. An article in the August 13, 1995, *Albert Lea Tribune* told of a letter dated 1948 from Paecher found by Shirley Hamer and her mother, Winnie. The article speculated whether the former prisoner was still alive.

Christiane Schieb of Albert Lea, a German war bride, saw the article. During a trip to her family home in Krefeld, Gemany, in January 1996, she took a copy of the *Tribune* article with her. She called directory assistance in the small city of Hofgeismer and asked for the telephone number of anyone with the name Wilhelm Paecher. She asked the man who answered if he had served in the German Army. He replied, "Yes." After more questions, it was established that Paecher was indeed the man who had worked on the Hamer farm as a POW. Contact was established after a lapse of fifty years, and letters have been exchanged between the Hamers and Paecher.

The last POW camp in Minnesota was Cut Foot Sioux, which was emptied on December 26, 1945. The prisoners were returned to Algona, Iowa, for repatriation. When those Germans departed, the camp at Algona was closed. The buildings were scrapped shortly afterward. Today the site of the former main prisoner of war camp is an airport.

This ended an unusual era in the annals of Minnesota history.

Bibliography

Ah La Ha Sa, published by the Students of Albert Lea High School, Albert Lea, Minnesota. November 16, 1944.

Albert Lea Evening Tribune, Albert Lea, Minnesota. Albert Lea Publishing Co., Paul C. Belknap, publisher. August 25, 1944; September 4, 1945.

Anderson, Chester G., editor *Growing Up in Minnesota,* University of Minnesota Press, Minneapolis. 1976.

Austin Daily Herald, Austin, Minnesota. H.R. Rasmussen, publisher. June 22, August 28, 29, October 19, 1944.

Bird Island Union, Bird Island, Minnesota. John K. Ploof, Publisher. August 31, September 21, 1944.

Clay County Historical Society Newsletter, March/April 1991, Vol. 14:2. Moorhead, Minnesota.

Cokato Enterprise, Cokato, Minnesota. Clifford L. Hedberg and Carlton E. Lee, publishers. August 3, 10, 24, 1944.

Contemporary Authors, 1969, Gail Research, Detroit, Michigan.

Crookston Daily Times, Crookston Times Printing Co., Crookston, Minnesota. P.A. McKenzie, president and editor. October 3, 5, 8, 12, 1945.

Daily People's Press, B.E. Darby & Sons, publishers. Owatonna, Minnesota. March 25, June 4, 29, 1944.

Deer River News, Deer River, Minnesota, A.L. La Freniere,

publisher. April 6, 27, June 22, 1944; Jan. 25, May 3, 31, 1945.

Drenth, John, Hollandale, Minnesota. Letters in possession of the author.

Duluth Herald, Victor R. Ridder, publisher, Duluth, Minnesota. November 11, 1943; April 16, October 30, November 2, 4, 1944.

Fairmont Daily Sentinel, Sentinel Publishing Co., Fairmont, Minnesota. Arthur M. Nelson, President. May 25, 27, June 4, 7, September 6, 28, October 3, November 30, December 1, 1944; March 12, 1945.

Fargo Forum and Daily Tribune, Fargo, North Dakota. June 6, 1944.

Faribault Daily News Republican and *Pilot,* Faribault Daily News, Inc. Faribault, Minnesota. July 5, 11, 1944.

Flandreau State Park History, coordinated by Archie Daleiden, Manager, in 1973.

Gaertner, Georg, with Arnold Krammer, *Hitler's Last Soldier in America,* 1985. Stein and Day, New York.

Grand Rapids Herald-Review, L.A. Rossman, publisher. Grand Rapids, Minnesota. February 2, April 12, October 11, 1944; January 17, May 16, December 26, 1945; May 22, 1972.

Hong, Howard. Personal interview May 24, 1995, at his home in Northfield, Minnesota.

Howard Lake Herald, Howard Lake, Minnesota. Owen A. Konchal, Olive M. Konchal, O. Edward Konchal, editors and publishers. August 3, 10, 17, 1944; July 12, August 9, 23, 1945.

Kraemer, Donald. *Nazi Prisoners of War in America,* 1979, Steen and Day, publishers, New York.

Land, The, Thursday, June 18, 1981. New Ulm, Carlienne Frisch, Editor. "German PW in Minnesota were Good Workers."

Lobdell, George H. "Minnesota's 1944 PW Escape," *Down the Mississippi in the Lili Marlene,* Minnesota History, fall, 1994. pp. 112 -123. Minnesota Historical Society, St. Paul, Minnesota.

Mankato Free Press, Mankato, Minnesota. Burtu Callahan, president; C. H. Russell, vice president and publisher. May 26, 27, 1944. March 11, 1991, James Richter, publisher.

Mathiowetz, Iris, Red Wing, Minnesota. Letter dated July 19, 1995, in the author's possession.

M209. Minnesota Historical Society film library. St. Paul, Minnesota. U.S. Army Provost Marshal General Reports on Prisoners of War 1942-1946.

M210. Minnesota Historical Society film library, St. Paul, Minnesota. U.S. Army Provost Marshal General Prisoners of War, Minnesota.

Minnesota Monthly. September 1983, 17\:9 Minnesota Historical Society, St. Paul, Minnesota.

Montgomery Messenger, Keohen and Sery, publishers, Montgomery, Minnesota. June 16, July 21, August 25, October 13, 1944.

Moorhead Daily News, J. Clark Dolliver, publisher, Moorhead, Minnesota. May 23, 29, 31, 1944.

New Ulm Daily Journal, (Brown County Journal). New Ulm, Minnesota. Walter K. Mickelson, publisher. May 16, June 1, 5, 9, 13; August 5, 25, October 2, 1944; August 6, 1975.

New Yorker Magazine, New York, New York. "Life in a Typical Prisoner of War Camp." February 20, 1944.

Norman County Index, Lightbrown Est. & Pfund. R.D. Pfund, business manager; E. F. Roesch, editor, Ada, Minnesota. October 11, 19, November 22, 1945.

Olivia Times Journal, Olivia, Minnesota. August 12, September 2, 16, October 28, 1943; September 6, 1945.

Ortonville Independent, L.A. Kaercher, editor and publisher, Ortonville, Minnesota. July 6, 18, 20, August 10, September 7, 1944.

Princeton Ledger, Princeton, Minnesota. Grace A. Dunn, publisher. September 2, 9, 23, November 4, 1943; August 31, September 21, October 5, 1944; August 23, 30, 1945.

Pluth, Edward J. "Prisoner of War Employment in Minnesota During World War," *Minnesota History,* No. 44, Winter, 1975. pp. 290-303. Minnesota Historical Society, St. Paul, Minnesota.

Reynen, Al and Doris, Hollandale, Minnesota. Letters in the author's possession.

Robins, Jim. "Minnesota Prisoner of War Camps," Mpls/St. Paul Magazine, MSP Publications, Minneapolis, Minnesota. January, 1986.

Rochester Post Bulletin, Rochester, Minnesota. Post Bulletin Company.

St. Charles Press, St. Charles, Minnesota. E.C. Clasen, and Lillian A. Clasen, publishers. June 1, 29, July 13, 1944; May 3, June 7, October 11, 1945; July 3, 1980.

St. Paul Pioneer Press, St. Paul, Minnesota. Joseph Ridder, Publisher. July 6, 1945; May 7, 1995.

Stillwater Evening Gazette, Stillwater, Minnesota, Mike Mahoney, publisher. December 17, 1996.

Stillwater Post Messenger, Stillwater, Minnesota, Stillwater Publishing Co., M.J. Brookman, president; R.A. Hannah, editor. February 14, 1946.

Timber Production War Project, U.S. Forest Service, Atlanta, Georgia.

Warren Sheaf, Mattson Brothers, Publishers, Warren, Minnesota. October 3, 10, 17, November 7, 1945.

Wells Mirror, E. Kuechenmeister, editor and manager. Wells, Minnesota. June 14, July 19, August 1, 1945.

"We Were the Lucky Ones." Taped Memorial Day, 1985. Minnesota Historical Society Audio Visual Collection Tape 4. Minnesota Historical Society, St. Paul, Minnesota.

Winona Daily News, "When German Nazis Lived in Winona County."

Zellmer, Blanche, Montgomery, Minnesota. Letter in author's possession.

Index